Leaders Who
Lead Successfully

Leaders Who Lead Successfully

Guidelines for Organizing to Achieve Innovation

Teruni Lamberg, Ph.D.

ROWMAN & LITTLEFIELD
Lanham • Boulder • New York • London

Published by Rowman & Littlefield
An imprint of The Rowman & Littlefield Publishing Group, Inc.
4501 Forbes Boulevard, Suite 200, Lanham, Maryland 20706
www.rowman.com

Unit A, Whitacre Mews, 26-34 Stannary Street, London SE11 4AB

British Library Cataloguing in Publication Information Available

Library of Congress Cataloging-in-Publication Data Available

Library of Congress Control Number: 2018938124

ISBN 978-1-4758-4133-6 (cloth: alk. paper)
ISBN 978-1-4758-4134-3 (pbk.: alk. paper)
ISBN 978-1-4758-4135-0 (electronic)

∞™ The paper used in this publication meets the minimum requirements of
American National Standard for Information Sciences—Permanence of Paper
for Printed Library Materials, ANSI/NISO Z39.48-1992.

Printed in the United States of America

To my wonderful parents, Kenneth and Shireen de Silva

My beloved Scott and Zack Lamberg

Contents

Preface

Do you have a burning desire to make a difference and improve things? Have you found yourself in a leadership position in your field? Perhaps you did not have leadership training as part of your education. Anyone can lead a team and keep things running. But how do you conceptualize a project that makes a difference and improves things?

When I joined the University of Nevada, Reno, the dean told me that this was a land-grant institution. Therefore, he expected my work to make an impact in the community. I had become an academic because I wanted to improve education. My work needed to make an impact in the community and the field of mathematics education. Therefore, I needed to explore the relationship between leadership and creativity.

Understanding creativity and the creative process is my lifelong passion because it is the secret of innovation. I have always been interested in how people become creative. I studied research on creativity because I wondered how people generate creative ideas and develop innovative products. At that time, I was a teacher and explored how to produce creativity in the classroom. I wrote a master's thesis on creative thinking.

When I was hired for a postdoctoral position at Vanderbilt University after I graduated with my doctorate in mathematics education, I found myself in a role of project manager, and very quickly I realized I needed to develop leadership skills to manage the project and generate new ideas. The whole purpose of being an academic was to make discoveries and come up with innovative new ideas in teams.

I realized that many people come out of college with disciplinary knowledge and have no clue how to lead a team. This included myself. This was when I began my journey of studying leadership research literature. The bottom line is that regardless of disciplinary learning, making a difference requires leadership skills. Most people find themselves in this role.

When I moved to Nevada, I became the principal investigator of Northeastern Nevada Mathematics Project and recently the Nevada Mathematics Project, a statewide effort with collaboration with every single school district in Nevada, Regional Training Centers, and six institutes of higher education. I had to admit that this was a massive undertaking. I knew that the success of the project depended on my leadership skills.

I felt the need to share what I learned because many people around the country and even worldwide kept asking me how I pulled this off. I embed my story throughout the book. I wanted to write a book that appealed not only to academics but also to anyone who intends to lead a team to innovate. Therefore, I present complex ideas in simple language that anyone can understand.

I was fortunate to be mentored by world-class leaders and interviewed them for this book. What a privilege to share their stories and insights on how they conceptualized problems, built a body of work over time, and organized teams. Understanding how successful leaders think, visualize a project, assemble a team, and learn together is necessary for a successful project. Furthermore, understanding how successful leaders have a vision and build a body of work over time is useful for understanding how to build a successful career.

This book documents research from my statewide research project, interviews from highly successful leaders whose work has made a national and international impact. It also contains interviews with influential K–12 leaders whose work had made an impact on their institutions. A leadership framework based on a review of research from business and other disciplines such as creativity is described.

The larger goal of this book is to understand how to conceptualize a project and organize a team so that the work makes a difference. In other words, learn how to lead a team to innovate for impact. I wrote another book titled *Conducting Productive Meetings: How to Generate and Communicate Ideas for Innovation* that is a companion book on how to run meetings to generate ideas, refine them, and innovate. Best wishes on your journey of organizing for innovation and making a difference!

Acknowledgments

I am thankful to everyone who inspired, encouraged, and supported me through this incredible journey of writing this book. This book represents many voices, stories, and insights that I am privileged to share. Thank you, Dr. James Barufaldi, Dr. Paul Cobb, Dr. Robert Chang, Mr. Priyan Fernando, Dr. Megan Franke, Dr. Rochelle Gutierrez, Dr. Kamil Jbeily, Dr. Richard Milner, and Dr. Mitchell Nathan for being my mentors and shaping my thinking. Your work has been innovative and made a national and international impact. Thank you for sharing your insights and experiences of leading teams to innovate.

Thank you, Mr. Dave Brancamp, Ms. Kathy Dees, Mr. David Ebert, Ms. Holly Marich, Ms. Marissa McClish, Ms. Jill Ross, Ms. Denise Trakas, and Ms. Sam Wutting. Your dedication to students is amazing, and you work tirelessly to make a difference in the lives of children. Thank you for sharing your wisdom about leading teams in a K–12 setting. You inspire me!

I would also like to thank the Nevada Mathematics Project team. What a journey to join in a statewide effort to improve STEM education in Nevada. Thank you Ms. Peggy Lakey, Dr. Edward Keppelman, Dr. Travis Olson, Dr. Jeff Shih, Dr. Ana de Bettencourt-Dias, Dr. Mathew Hsu, Ms. Gail Hunt, Dr. Barbara Perez, Ms. Tina Westwood, Dr. Rebecca Bondocco, Dr. Diana Moss, Dr. Steven Demelin, Ms. Lucy Gillette, Ms. Tina Westwood, Ms. Sarah Negrete, Ms. Kirsten Gleissner, the Nevada Department of Education (Dave Brancamp, Ms. Tracy Gruber, Mr. Mike Pacheco, and Dr. Heather Crawford-Ferre), and regional training centers (Dr. Kirsten Gleissner, Dr. Sarah Negrete, Ms. Chelli Smith, and Ms. Kathy Dees) in Nevada. We were fortunate to get the support from *all* school districts in the state of Nevada and also the support of some private and charter schools. It is a privilege to work with you. Thank you to the graduate student research team, Mrs. Linda Gillette-Kogen, Dr. Claudia Bertolone-Smith, and Mr. Zachary Kirkwood.

Many people read through the manuscript and provided thoughtful feedback that helped shape the book. Dr. Craig Wall, thank you for helping me conceptualize this book and providing thoughtful comments throughout the writing process. Ms. Elaine Pohle provided critical and timely feedback on my writing. Mr. Charlie Arroyo, I am grateful for the feedback you provided from a business perspective.

I would also like to thank all the innovative leaders that I interviewed who took time to read the manuscript and provide thoughtful feedback. Thank you, Ms. Denise Trakas, for your suggestion of including the section on K–12 voices and providing thoughtful comments. Thank you, Ms. Marrissa McClish, for your thoughts and recommendations. I also appreciate the support of Mr. Steve Harrison's group for their mentoring, especially Ms. Debra Englander and Ms. Martha Bullen. Thank you, Mr. Tom Koerner, my editor, who provided support and encouraging words throughout the writing process. A special thank you to Ms. Carlie Wall and Ms. Ashleigh Cooke from Rowman & Littlefield.

I am thankful for the love and support of my parents. They live a life that involves serving others. A special thank you to my husband, Scott, and my son, Zack, who was always there for me with a warm smile and a sense of humor. I love you.

Introduction

Why Study Leadership?

If your actions inspire others to dream more, learn more, do more, and become more, you are a leader.

—*John Quincy Adams*

One of the great myths in life is that studying hard, getting good grades, and learning a discipline well will lead to success. However, making a difference in this world requires something more. Leadership skills are needed to motivate others, harness resources, and come up with innovative ideas to achieve extraordinary things. Very rarely can an individual accomplish great things in isolation! People who make a difference don't do it alone. They know how to lead teams to innovate.

Innovation is the ability to come up with new ideas and better ways of doing things to improve the human condition. This is the reason why new products and services get developed. Our economy today is knowledge based. Therefore, innovation is an important part of advancing knowledge and improving things. Katherine Graham-Leviss wrote an article for the *Harvard Business Review*. She pointed out that even though innovation is critical, it is also difficult to cultivate quality innovative leaders.

Therefore, there is a need to understand how to lead teams to innovate. We need to know what innovation is and how to develop as a leader who can lead a team to innovate. We don't live in a perfect world. Regardless of context, when challenges arise, great leaders take the initiative. They seize the opportunity to inspire others and innovate.

For example, Elon Reeve Musk has an incredible track record of leading innovation. He immigrated to the United States from South Africa and went from being broke to becoming a millionaire by the age of twenty-eight. When many people were still using the phone book, he had the vision to digitize the phone book and newspapers so that people could find information online. He envisioned this in the 1980s when computers were just emerging in the market. He formed the Zip2 Company, which he sold to Compaq Computer Corporation for over $300 million. He did not stop there; he continued to move on to his next "big idea."

Elon Musk is driven by figuring out what he is going to do next, explained Max Chafkin, a writer for *Bloomberg BusinessWeek*. Max Chafkin interviewed Elon Musk when he was a writer for *Inc.* magazine. He pointed out that Musk has a desire to change the world. He said that Musk jumped quickly to the next project without much time lag despite the fact he could have retired and lived a very comfortable life.[1] Musk went on to form PayPal.

In his interview, Musk told Chafkin that he wanted to "create a company in the financial sector that will have a profound effect."[2] He formed a company called Xdot.com, which made it possible to do electronic transfers as opposed to mailing checks. He later founded SpaceX to figure out how to get to space cheaply. In 1994, he launched Tesla, the first auto industry start-up. In 2017 *Forbes Magazine* listed it as the number 1 innovative company.

Leaders who lead teams to innovate have unique qualities. They not only motivate people to act but also know how to create the right conditions for innovative thinking to take place. They inspire and empower their team to push the boundaries of their thinking. They have a vision. They know how to communicate their vision, gather resources, and work with people. They know how to put a team together and get them excited to accomplish extraordinary things.

They are forward thinking and live a life that pushes their boundaries as well as those of their team. Curiosity and purpose drive their actions. They are not just managers who keep things running. Their body of work builds on each other. They have a vision, a passion, and a love of what they are doing. An interesting part of innovative leaders is that the leader has a depth of understanding of a field, and also an interdisciplinary background that allows them to be creative and lead a team.

Interestingly, these leaders have a larger 360-degree view of things. They can see the "big picture" of how things fit together and connect. They are visionaries who can visualize possibilities in the future. An innovative leader is like an artist. It is a way of life. As they work on a project, they imagine and visualize the possibilities of how this can lead to future work.

They are also thinking about how they can solve problems in society and make the world a better place. They understand the needs of the community they serve. They know how to navigate constraints and solve problems that arise. They know how to garner resources and to work within constraints.

LEADERSHIP SKILLS ARE NEEDED TO MAKE A DIFFERENCE!

> Unlike business thinking, innovative thinking doesn't rely on past experiences of known facts. It imagines a desired future state and how to get there. It is intuitive and open to possibility.
>
> —David Magellan Horth and Jonathan Vehar,
> Center for Creative Leadership

Leadership skills sometimes develop out of necessity to accomplish things. Perhaps this might be the case for you. Dr. James Barufaldi served as the director of the Center for STEM Education at the University of Texas at Austin, and as a principal investigator for the Texas Regional Collaborative for Excellence in Science Teaching. He shared his thoughts about leadership:

> First of all, I never wanted or set out to be a leader. I never wanted to have an administrative role. I was perfectly happy in my classroom, teaching and researching so on. I just fell into it and got involved in a leadership position. And when you just asked me about leadership, I thought it was interesting because I started to think about what it takes to be a good strong leader. I think, I have been very well-known to be optimistic. Some people claim that I look at the world through "rose-colored glasses."[3]

The interesting point he made is that he has a very optimistic view of the world. This optimism influenced his desire to accomplish things to make a difference. He believed that accomplishing great things was possible. His Center for STEM Education served the entire state of Texas and beyond. His current work involves working overseas. He cares deeply about helping teachers become better science teachers and learning from research. He loved going into classrooms and working with teachers. Therefore, his desire to serve others required leadership skills to accomplish his higher purpose.

Making a difference through leadership can sometimes make a large impact, such as the work done by Dr. Barufaldi, or it can even make a difference in a smaller setting. For example, it might involve coming up with better ways to figure out how to assess what students are thinking and use that information to teach more effectively. Perhaps a principal can lead a group of teachers to optimize how they use curriculum for maximum impact. It does not matter what field you work in; leadership skills are needed to make a difference and come up with better ways to do things. Great ideas can develop in teams under the right conditions.

The following section provides a rationale for studying leadership to make a difference. The sections that follow describe characteristics of an effective leader who can lead teams to innovate. These features include having a vision and being able to inspire others into action. It also includes seizing opportunities for innovation, developing a body of work over time, and having a quest for excellence and perfection.

The good news is that leadership skills can be developed. We can learn from innovative leaders who have led teams to come up with extraordinary results. Many years ago, I started studying business literature because I wondered how leaders ran teams to innovate. I had joined Vanderbilt University as a postdoctoral researcher and was part of a research team in mathematics education.

As a research team, we were expected to make discoveries and come up with new and innovative ideas. Even though I had disciplinary knowledge in mathematics education, I realized that I needed leadership skills to make a difference. Therefore, I studied research on innovation and leadership and interviewed world-class researchers who have successfully led teams to innovate and make an impact on society.

I wanted to know how a team could work together to come up with innovative ideas. The research team of scholars worked with teachers and administrators in school districts around the country. Even though many of us came out of college with a specialized degree, many of us have not taken a leadership course. Making a real difference that affects people's lives involves the ability to identify real problems and generate innovative solutions. This process involves working with interdisciplinary teams. You don't even need a college degree to gain leadership skills.

Leadership skills are necessary to innovate and lead a team to get extraordinary results. Think about what you are trying to accomplish and what kind of leadership skills are needed to achieve your goals.

My curiosity and interest about creativity and innovation emerged when I was nineteen and a young preschool teacher. I started my first job and decided to teach young children. Previously, I had worked as a teaching assistant in my mother's Montessori school and discovered that many young children have a natural curiosity and a love of learning. I had moved to Arizona and taken a job as a preschool teacher. At that point, I did not have any formal training as a preschool teacher other than the job experiences I had at my mother's school.

I was so surprised when I was asked not to stimulate children's minds with learning. My job was to help children socialize and not teach them anything. This request did not make sense to me because the kids loved learning and enjoyed being in my class.

I worked in another preschool that devalued art. Those children were limited to drawing on a five-by-five-inch sheet of paper and were not allowed to share their work in the classroom. These experiences made me wonder why people did things that did not make sense. My journey to understand how to create conditions for creativity and innovation started at this young age.

As I became an elementary teacher, I explored how to cultivate conditions for creativity in the classroom. I studied creativity as part of my master's work. As a result, I ended up winning many teaching awards. Later, when I became a researcher, I realized that combining creativity and innovation with leadership is essential for coming up with innovative ideas and discovering new things that make an impact in society.

Very rarely are things innovated in isolation. Rather, working with teams is an essential part of innovation. That is why I interviewed eight world-renowned researchers and a business leader who have successfully led teams to innovate and make an impact in their communities. I am fortunate enough to know these people. They have touched and shaped my thinking in many ways. I share their stories on how they implemented the leadership principles.

In addition, stories from K–12 leaders who have made significant contributions to K–12 education are provided in chapter 5 in the section titled "Voices from the Field: Innovative K–12 Leader Interviews." These leaders share insights on leadership principles outlined in this book as experienced in the field. These leadership principles are not limited to the field of education. They can work in any setting where you are leading a team to be productive and innovate.

The four research-based leadership principals outlined in this book will help you become a transformative leader who can lead a team to innovate. You will be inspired to explore who you are and what you value and figure out ways to realize your dreams. These insights will help you put together and lead a team to get extraordinary results. It will help you become a visionary leader who can lead a team to innovate.

The leadership principles outlined in this book can be used in any context, not just education. It could be in a small or large setting depending on the goals and purpose. The bottom line is that these principles can be used by anyone who wants to lead a team to innovate regardless of context.

The *four leadership principles* outlined in this book will guide you to make decisions on how to conceptualize a problem and assemble and lead a team to innovate. World-renowned scholars have used these research-based principals to achieve extraordinary results. Their stories will inspire you. You will learn about how they led teams to innovate. In addition, K–12 innovative leaders share how they used the principles in action.

I share my story of the Nevada Mathematics Project. This is the beginning of a journey of transforming mathematics education in Nevada. The work is still in progress, and we still have a long way to go! But we made great strides in coming together as a state. The principles are strategies that you can use, and the reflection questions throughout the book will motivate you to act.

Think About . . .

> ➤ What leadership experiences have you had? What worked or did not work?
> ➤ How can you draw from these experiences to help you lead teams to do innovative things?

A GREAT LEADER HAS VISION AND INSPIRES ACTION

A leader inspires others to act by communicating a vision by connecting with hearts and minds.

—Teruni Lamberg

A great leader is one who can motivate and inspire others to act to do extraordinary things. An article written by Prentice in the *Harvard Business Review* pointed out that a good leader motivates people to act.[4] Also, the leader understands what drives people individually and collectively.

Think About . . .

> ➤ Think about some leaders who inspire you. What characteristics do they have? What is their leadership style? How do they inspire a team to innovate?

Steve Jobs, the founder of Apple, is described as a "visionary" and "unconventional leader." Sarah NcInerney, who wrote an article in *Executive Style* online magazine described him as a visionary leader whose leadership style was more of a "high maintenance co-worker." She further added that Steve Jobs demanded excellence from his staff.[5] Also, he was known for his blunt delivery of criticism.

What was unique about Jobs's leadership was his ability to bring his team, investors, and customers along on the journey. He communicated his vision and inspired others to follow. Steve Jobs did not complete college; in fact, he was a dropout. A college degree is not a requirement for becoming a visionary leader.

The innovations that Apple has made are incredible! Who would have ever dreamed of someday being able to chat on the phone through a watch! Great leaders develop their vision during the early stages of their careers and build on it over time. Sometimes it involves imagining things and possibilities that do not exist. For example, Steve Jobs started his company with only $1,300 and made it to the Fortune 500 company list by 1983. Imagining the potential of what you want to accomplish long term is an important part of the journey of a visionary leader who leads a team to innovate.

Several years ago, I met H. Richard Milner IV (also known as Rich) at Vanderbilt University. Rich had graduated from college and was a new faculty member at Vanderbilt University. He was a wonderful friend and a source of comfort and support. We had a connection because we were both new and were trying to navigate academia. It was an exciting time and a little bit scary too because the future was unknown.

We both had to imagine our career paths. We were both in a research institution that had high demands. I remember one day sitting in his office chatting. He had a whiteboard on the wall next to his desk. He took a marker and made a diagram of his vision for the future. He wanted to be an expert in diversity and help underserved children.

I remember him giving me advice about having a focused research agenda. These words influenced my future work. In other words, I needed to define "who I was and what I wanted to achieve." I realized that I needed to identify my goals and stay focused to achieve them. That day I also realized the value of finding mentors who I could ask for advice.

I just got off the phone talking to Dr. Richard Milner as I was writing this book. It had been fifteen years since we both sat in his office discussing what we wanted to accomplish. I pointed out to Rich, "Do you remember us chatting and you writing on the whiteboard?" He laughed and replied, "Yes, I remember that day." I told him, "Well, you accomplished what you set out to do!"

Rich serves as the director of the Center for Urban Education at the University of Pittsburgh. He is a well-respected scholar who has published several books and articles on diversity issues. In 2017, *Education Week* ranked him as one of the most influential scholars on their education list for influencing policy and practice. It warmed my heart to see where he is now.

Think About . . .

➢ Close your eyes and imagine the possibilities! Think outside the box. Imagination is an important part of being a visionary leader. If you can't imagine it, you certainly cannot achieve it!

INNOVATIVE LEADERS SEIZE OPPORTUNITIES FOR INNOVATION

Innovative leaders seize opportunities and take the initiative to lead teams to innovate regardless of context. They view challenges as opportunities to come up with new solutions. Kouzes and Posner, who wrote the book *Leadership Challenge*, gave an example of a Starbucks store manager using her blender to make drinks that later became a hit with customers.

She did this because the store did not want to invest in blenders. Eventually, Starbucks invested in the drink because the demand was high. These authors pointed out that the important takeaway is that great leaders allow team members to take the initiative and solve problems. They particularly find the right challenge to inspire others to engage.[6]

Jeffrey Baumgartner, the author of the book *The Way of the Innovation Master*, points out that innovative leaders do need to have expertise in the area that they are trying to innovate.[7] Therefore, matching expertise with leadership is necessary. A white paper written by David Horth and Dan Buchner for the Center for Creative Leadership pointed out that innovative leadership has two components: (1) the innovative leader who applies creative thinking to leadership tasks, as in the example of the Starbucks manager, and (2) leading for innovation that involves working with others to support them to innovate.[8]

LEADERS DEVELOP A BODY OF KNOWLEDGE OVER TIME

Leadership skills develop over an individual's career. Dr. Robert Chang, the center director of materials research at Northwestern University, had an incredible history of accomplishing great things in the field of nanotechnology. He shared with me that he developed his amazing body of work over time. He said, "It did not happen overnight but over time." Accomplishing extraordinary things involves having a long-term vision of the future while working on short-term goals.

I remember sitting in project meetings at Vanderbilt, so excited to work with a rock star in the mathematics education world. This rock star was Dr. Paul Cobb, a world-renowned math education researcher whose work is known internationally. He is even a member of the National Academies of Education. I remember him telling us about the importance of having your work build over time instead of starting and stopping. This way, ideas can be refined over time.

Each project is a jumping-off point for the next great idea. It is a body of work that builds over time. Paul was curious about how students think and learn. His work built on individual teaching experiments expanded to classroom research. Then he branched out into working with teachers and providing professional development and ultimately working with school districts at scale. He inspired and motivated a whole team of graduate students and me as the postdoctoral candidate.

One of the things that motivated or influenced his work was a curiosity to know more, to understand, to make a difference in the classroom for kids. The lesson to learn here is that leadership for innovation is a journey that you refine and build over time. It also involves thinking about a body of work over time to keep innovating.

Think About . . .

➤ Leaders develop over time. It involves being true to yourself.
➤ What is your vision?

VISIONARY LEADERS HAVE A QUEST FOR EXCELLENCE

Excellence is never an accident. It is always a result of high intention, sincere effort, and intelligent execution. It represents the wise choice of many alternatives. Choice, not chance, determines your destiny.

—Aristotle

The pursuit of excellence drives visionary leaders who lead teams to innovate. They demand excellence not only from others but also from themselves. People are driven to follow visionary leaders to be part of something bigger. People followed Steve Jobs because of his quest for excellence, and he expected that from people. People like to be challenged and to push their boundaries.

McInerney pointed out that being focused and disciplined sets the stage for accomplishing great things.[9] The path to excellence is not always smooth. There are bumps along the way. It is working through these hard times that paves the way for accomplishing even greater things. Visionary leaders are also good mentors and set the example of excellence for themselves. They may have high expectations for their team, but they expect that from themselves as well. Even though they have busy lives, they manage their time and provide quick feedback to their teams.

I experienced with Dr. Paul Cobb and Dr. Robert Chang the pursuit of excellence. I found myself revising and revisiting the data multiple times and being challenged to push my thinking by Dr. Cobb. I was working with Dr. Chang writing a National Science Foundation grant. He stayed late hours giving me feedback almost immediately as I was writing a draft.

Both Dr. Cobb and Dr. Chang always responded very quickly to e-mails as I was working on things. The timeliness of feedback was critical for doing high-quality work. They both gave very detailed feedback that allowed me to keep improving what I was doing. Their communication was almost instantaneous. They demanded high-quality work. However, they worked just as hard as I did. Even though I was exhausted at times working long hours late into the night, I was also motivated to do the task because I was part of something bigger. I was also grateful for their mentoring. Their energy and focus are inspirational.

Characteristics of Successful Innovative Leaders/Scholars

- They have good leadership skills, and their work makes an impact in society by solving real problems.
- Their body of work solves a real need.
- They have a vision and inspire a team to act.
- They seize opportunities for innovation.
- They develop a body of knowledge over time.
- They have a quest for excellence.

HOW TO USE THIS BOOK

The purpose of this book is to help the reader learn how to identify a problem, assemble a project team, create conditions for innovation, and lead a team for extraordinary results. Therefore, anyone who wants to lead a team to innovate will find this book useful. For example, it is intended for teacher leaders, coaches, principals, academics, program coordinators, business individuals, and others. This book is about how to make a difference by solving real-world problems and coming up with innovative solutions. The following key ideas will be addressed throughout this volume:

- How to identify a problem to solve
- How to assemble an interdisciplinary team to solve problems
- How to capitalize on the team's expertise and strengths
- How to create conditions to generate ideas

The following topics are addressed in the companion book, *Conducting Successful Meetings: How to Generate and Communicate Ideas for Innovation* (2018).

- How to engage a team in creative problem-solving
- How to run meetings to move the project agenda forward

- How to consider the needs and context of how the innovation will be used by the end user to improve design
- How to effectively communicate with the project team and stakeholders

These research-based principles can be used by anyone who is interested in leading a team to innovate for impact. Each principle is illustrated with examples of how world-renowned scholars led teams to innovate as well as K–12 leaders. In addition, the author describes a case study of the Nevada Mathematics Project, which she leads to illustrate the principles in action.

Each chapter contains key principles, examples of these principles in action, self-reflection strategies, and action items that can be implemented right away. The book can be used as a toolbox to meet the reader's needs to lead a highly productive project team and innovate.

The chapters are organized as follows: Chapter 1 is about discovering the leader's purpose and values to define a problem. Chapters 2, 3, and 4 describe how to assemble, interact, and bond as a team. Detailed biographies of the innovative leaders interviewed are listed in chapter 5 as a reference. Any person leading a project team to be productive and innovate can use this book. Chapter 5 also contains innovative K–12 leader interviews that illustrate how the principles outlined in the book can be used in a K–12 educational setting.

Several tools are provided in this book so that the ideas can be pragmatically implemented to run a successful project. "Think About" reflection questions are provided throughout the chapters for the reader to reflect on their own work and make connections. The "Action Items" sections provide concrete strategies that can be adapted to lead a project team. In addition, a summary of key ideas is provided at the end of each chapter.

NOTES

1. Max Chafkin, *Eccentric Billionaire Elon Musk from Zero to Hero*, interview of Elon Musk, 2017.

2. Chafkin, *Eccentric Billionaire Elon Musk*.

3. Dr. James Barufaldi, interview by Teruni Lamberg. All quotations of Dr. Barufaldi in this book are from this interview.

4. W. C. H. Prentice, "Organizational Culture, Understanding Leadership," *Harvard Business Review* (online version from January 2004).

5. Sarah McInerney, "Steve Jobs: An Unconventional Leader," *Executive Style*, 2011, www.executivestyle.com.au/steve-jobs-an-unconventional-leader-1lcmo.

6. James Kouzes and Barry Posner, *Leadership Challenge: How to Make Extraordinary Things Happen in Organizations*, 5th ed. (San Francisco: Jossey-Bass, 2012).

7. Jeffrey Baumgartner, *The Way of the Innovation Master* (Erps-Kwerps, Belgium: JPB Bwiti, 2010).

8. David Magellan Horth and D. Buchner, *White Paper on Innovative Leadership: How to Use Innovation to Lead Effectively, Work Collaboratively and Drive Results,* 2015, www.ccl.org/wp-content/uploads/2015/04/InnovationLeadership.pdf.

9. McInerney, "Steve Jobs."

ONE

How to Build an Action Plan

Twenty years from now you will be more disappointed by the things that you didn't do than by the ones you did do. So, throw off the bowlines. Sail away from the safe harbor. Catch the trade winds in your sails. Explore. Dream. Discover.

—Mark Twain

An innovative leader has a strong sense of self and beliefs. A leader's passion inspires others to act. Passion comes from deep within. For example, Dr. Richard Milner shared that he deeply values his African American roots and upbringing. He cares deeply about *all* students: "particularly about students who are underserved, who are mistreated and labeled as deficient."[1] He was referring to students who live below the poverty line, black and brown students, or students who have a disability. "My work is tied to my mission of improving life chances of these students."

He shared that he was so proud of his family members. His parents were just ordinary folks who did not have a college education but were brilliant people who inspired him. He could see their humanity and talent. He honored their brilliance, and it made him sensitive to think about other people. Rich shared: "The journey that brought me here is that my parents were blue-collar workers. My dad drove a forklift for 39 years, and mom was a hairdresser: They were high school graduates—no college for them."

He added, "The other piece, I have tried to look at is doing work with my heart and head. I think that is one of the things that separates me." He explained that "it allowed me to have a vision so that I can provide educational opportunities to meet their needs." Living a life where his daily work is consistent with his vision is important to Rich to be a successful leader.

Dr. Rochelle Gutiérrez had a similar story. She had originally planned to go to medical school and went to Stanford for her undergraduate degree. She was doing everything to pursue medicine and become a

1

pediatrician. In many ways, she felt that this was an expected role for her because she wanted to invest in her community and improve the health care offered to Latinx families. However, realizing that she was always tutoring other students in mathematics in her free time, there was something deep inside her that made her passionate about social justice issues related to mathematics education.

She shared that a Stanford professor made her rethink her career path. A realization came upon her that she needed to work in education because it was a difficult choice and not an expected choice. She had experienced social justice issues as a Latina student navigating academia.

When asked to think about what shaped her strong passion, she grew quiet for a moment as she reflected on this question. She thought about it and remarked that her upbringing shaped her thinking. She grew up in a family that was deeply involved in activism and social justice. She shared with me that like Dr. Milner, she was driven by her desire to make a difference and serve her Latinx community.

She takes her work very seriously because it impacts lives! She recognizes the responsibility that comes with a career that can change and transform lives. She wants to empower teachers and give them the tools to be advocates for children within the school system. Her research focuses on preservice teachers' knowledge and dispositions to teach powerful mathematics to students for whom the schooling system has historically failed. She, too, mentioned that her beliefs, actions, and lifestyle must align.

Her work with the community and schools is an important part of her mission. When you meet Rochelle, you see the passion in her eyes along with her radiant smile. Dr. Rochelle Gutiérrez is a professor of mathematics education in curriculum and instruction at the University of Illinois at Urbana-Champaign. She won numerous awards for her work in mathematics education in the area of equity. Her passions powerfully shaped her research agenda:

> I guess when I think about leadership, I think about leading by example. If I would say that I am a leader, I feel that I don't just talk the talk; I feel that I live what I expect other people to do or understand. At the level of the researcher, there are particular things that I do, and I feel that I stand by those. . . .
>
> I have to look at myself in the mirror and always come back to the internal compass of "Why am I doing what I am doing? Who does my work benefit?" And when I am able to come back to that and hold myself accountable, I am also modeling to other people. It is not to just say that these things are important in your research, but that you actually do them on a regular basis as you move through life. And, who you are in life is not separate from research.[2]

John Maxwell, who wrote the book *21 Irrefutable Laws of Leadership*, states that the bottom line of leadership is *influence*. *Passion* is an essential part of being able to influence others for a cause. Therefore, drawing from your passions to lead teams will inspire others to follow.[3] The next section will help you identify what you are passionate about by reflecting on your personal story.

DISCOVER WHO YOU ARE BY REFLECTING ON YOUR JOURNEY

To find yourself, think for yourself.

—Socrates

Who are you? What is your life story? What is important to you? These are important questions that shape who you are and your passions. The bottom line is that leading for innovation is a way of life. In a moment, I am going to ask you to think deeply about your life and your journey. Who you are defines what you do, and how others respond. Your life story is unique and personal to you. Think about your life journey and what matters to you.

For example, when I reflected on my life journey, I realized what shaped my thinking. My journey began working for my mother. She owns Montessori schools in Austin, Texas. During my late teen years when attending college, I worked part-time as a teaching assistant. I found myself drawn to working with the little ones. They were always delighted to discover new things and had such a sense of wonder. Their sparkling eyes and smiles warmed my heart.

I moved to Arizona and became an elementary teacher. When I was in the classroom, it was magical. My students inspired me. I loved them like my children. I was a very young teacher back then and felt like a novice. So I kept taking more and more classes at Arizona State University to become a better teacher.

The love of my students motivated me to keep learning. I wanted to inspire them to think and be creative. The kids were so motivated to learn. When I arrived to set up my classroom early, there were usually about ten kids lined up wanting to enter the classroom to work on their projects. They were so engaged by what they were doing. Squeals of laughter and wonder filled the room. I loved every minute of it.

At this point in my life, I was not married and did not have any children. I decided that my life work would be to make a difference in children's lives. I ended up pursuing a Ph.D. in mathematics education while teaching. I applied what I had learned in my classes at night during the day with my students. When faced with the fact of graduating, a realization came over me that I was giving up a job that involved working with children that I loved.

As I reflected on my situation, it dawned on me that I could make a greater difference in the lives of many children. I had the opportunity to support teachers. My deepest desire is to help children succeed. My graduate work has focused specifically on teaching math. I was starting a new adventure. I was delighted to get a postdoctorate position with Dr. Paul Cobb at Vanderbilt University, who is a world-renowned math education researcher.

He is part of the National Academies of Education and known as one of the most influential minds in mathematics education. I was going to soak up learning from him. He was working on a project in two different states across the country to support teachers to become better math teachers. My goal was (and still is) to make a difference in lives of children. If I wanted to help children, then I needed to support teachers.

Figure out who you are and what you stand for. This way you know what is important to you and what you believe in your heart. John Kotter, the author of *Leading Change*, points out that developing a vision as a leader is a matter of both head and heart.[4] Chapter 2 outlines how you can do this.

Think About . . .

  ➤ Think about your personal journey. Jot down some key events in your life that define you.
  ➤ Write down who you are and what you stand for. What are you passionate about?

Take a moment to think about your life story. Who are you? What is important to you, and what do you value? What contribution do you want to make in this world? Once you have identified your purpose, think about your core values.

Think About . . .

  ➤ What are your core values?
  ➤ What do you stand for?

Developing a vision for your life requires thinking about your higher values and goals. Jack Canfield, the coauthor of *The Success Principles: How to Get from Where You Are to Where You Want to Be*, also points out how important it is to know who you are and figure out your life purpose. He writes that when you live a life that is aligned with your life purpose, you automatically end up helping others.[5]

ALIGN YOUR ACTIONS WITH YOUR CORE VALUES: WALK THE TALK

Your core values are what you deeply believe in that influences your decisions and actions.

—Teruni Lamberg

Align your actions with your core values. What are your core values? You need to understand what these are to lead a team to innovate and make a difference. It does not matter who you are or what you do; you have something deeper inside you that matters to you! When you align your core values and goals, you can pursue all opportunities and possibilities that come your way.

Bill George, the author of *Discover Your True North*, describes this as your "True North." He viewed deeply held values and principles as a leader's compass that guides decision-making.[6] Therefore, being cognizant of your principles and deeply held values is essential to making decisions that matter. Otherwise, a leader might find him- or herself floundering without a purpose or direction.

Dr. Milner and Dr. Gutiérrez shared that it was important for them to live a life that reflected their values. It is not about emulating someone else. Bill George points out that you should draw power from your life story, which gives you passion and the compassion to lead.[7] Kouzes and Posner, in their book *Leadership Challenge*, as well as Bill George, point out the importance of finding your voice.[8] They explain that being consistent in your words and deeds is important for having integrity and ultimately influence. That leadership is about finding your voice and defining and living your values

Core values should become an inner compass to drive decisions and actions. An authentic leader is someone whose beliefs and actions are aligned. It is only then that a leader can inspire and lead others to make a difference or come up with innovative and creative solutions! For example, Dr. James Barufaldi, the Ruben E. Hinojosa Regents Professor, director of the Center for STEM Education, and principal investigator for the Texas Regional Collaborative for Excellence in Science Teaching (TRC), strongly feels that an important character trait a leader needs is *trustworthiness.*

Sibyl Kaufman wrote an article on Dr. Barufaldi and stated that peers and students describe him as the "Godfather of STEM."[9] He has an impressive list of scholarships and awards for his work and has made a difference in Texas and beyond. Furthermore, he was very influential in developing University of Texas at Austin as one of the leading institutions in STEM education. Dr. Barufaldi describes the importance of *trustworthiness* below:

> I have known leaders who never developed that. People just did not trust that person for many reasons. Maybe it was personality, attitude, or whatever. But I have seen leaders who would walk into a situation within an organization and would immediately establish that *trustworthiness* within and among the organization, which I was really impressed with.

It also became very apparent that Dr. Barufaldi deeply cared about serving his community and addressing real needs. An *optimistic viewpoint* was one of his core values. He explained that he sees the world through "rose-colored glasses." He thinks anything is possible, and he looks for the good in people and situations. His optimistic viewpoint influences everything he does. Optimism affects how he interacts with people and his body of work. Also, his optimism allowed him to transcend any failures or negativity:

> Who you are is what goes into that research. What needs to be improved or solved? Who you are really plays a role in that. I have always been a very optimistic person. I always knew the results [would] be encouraging, even if it was weak or negative. I found a way to make it more positive. A good leader is always a risk taker. The majority of them were very successful. When I started out, I failed miserably. It takes a strong-minded person to be a good risk taker.

Kouzes and Posner, the authors of *Leadership Challenge: How to Make Extraordinary Things Happen in Organizations*, also point out that clarifying your values is an important part of being an effective leader.[10] Your thoughts and actions should communicate these values. Bill George and others point out that aligning your higher values with your goals of what you want to accomplish is critical to success.[11] Now that you have figured out who you are, and your core values, it is time to visualize the goals that you would like to achieve. Developing leadership skills and becoming a great leader is a lifelong journey.

VISUALIZE THE POSSIBILITIES!

Go ahead and stretch your imagination; anything is possible! You need to imagine it before you can achieve it.

—Teruni Lamberg

What are your dreams? Don't hold back; think big! Anything is possible! Dreaming big dreams is an important part of your journey as a leader. The ability to imagine and visualize the possibilities is important. What is unique about Elon Musk is that he could visualize and imagine a future without being constrained by the current context. At that time, the Yellow Pages phone book was a very significant part of American society. People used the gigantic phone book to find information. This is how people did things. He visualized a future that involved changing traditional behaviors. He imagined a future that did not exist at that point.

When I first interviewed in Nevada for a job as an assistant professor, the then-dean told me that he would like me to move there to make a math education presence in Nevada. At that point, there was very limited work being done in the community in mathematics education. Furthermore, there was a lack of financial and human resources to carry out the work.

The state was vast, and there was insufficient communication across the different geographic areas. At this point, I needed to decide. I was in the process of completing a postdoctorate position at Vanderbilt University. Do I go to a place with many resources and support or take on the challenge of making a difference? Therefore, I needed to imagine the possibilities to carry out the work that the dean had proposed.

I needed to dream big. I had never traveled through Nevada to understand its unique and diverse geography and cities. Furthermore, I was not a native Nevadan; I had a diverse background. I needed to cultivate the relationships and the resources to make that happen. The possibilities were exciting and a little scary too.

Dreaming big dreams requires taking risks and moving forward! It also involves an optimistic viewpoint to consider that the possibilities can be a reality. Furthermore, it involves visualizing possibilities that do not currently exist. Therefore, do not think about constraints; instead, open yourself up to possibilities, and think outside the box. Dr. Barufaldi said the following about visualizing the impossible:

> You can always make it possible. I have this vision of the Texas Regional Collaborative that we learned and I am trying to think of ways that good things happen when you have strong professional development. . . .
> Where do you get that from? I get that because it is my rose-colored lens [laughs].

The TRC became a statewide effort that Dr. Kamil A. Jbeily founded at the Texas Education Agency, and which later moved to the University of Texas of Austin with Dr. Barufaldi serving at its principal investigator. Dr. Barufaldi and Dr. Jbeily were both instrumental in shaping my thinking and helping me visualize a statewide effort in Nevada.

Think About . . .

> ➤ Visualize what you would like to see happen. Don't hold back!
> ➤ Think outside the box of what is possible!

FIND INTERESTING CHALLENGES TO SOLVE

The Formulation of a problem is often more essential than its solution, which may be merely a matter of mathematical or experimental skills.

—Albert Einstein

Leaders who make extraordinary things happen are constantly thinking about the "next new idea" and seize opportunities that come their way or even create them. They enjoy tackling interesting problems because they find the challenge intrinsically interesting. It is this interest and a desire to be challenged with interesting problems that drive their passions and actions to motivate others. Each challenge or project they work on is a stepping stone for the next best idea!

Kouzes and Posner point out that leaders actively seek out problems to solve as opposed to waiting for "fate to smile on them."[12] Effective leaders are learners; they are observers and risk-takers with an optimistic attitude. Ultimately, they can get teams together based on their initial vision and co-create a team vision. Understanding how successful leaders come up with interesting problems or challenges to solve can be helpful when thinking about how to come up with new project ideas.

The leaders interviewed in this book spent a lot of time observing and listening to the community they were serving. They got multiple perspectives and studied the topic. The interesting point is that they were constantly thinking about the people that they were serving. Specifically, they examined their needs and ways they could help. The goal was to come up with novel solutions to creative problems.

This process is like the design process used by IDEO. IDEO is an influential product-development firm in the Silicon Valley. This company develops many products such as the first mouse for the computer or squishy handles on a toothbrush. They take the ordinary and make it better by using their design principles. Dan Rather created a TV documentary of how this design process worked. In this episode, the team was tasked to redesign a better shopping cart in five days.[13]

Tom Kelly documented this design process in his book *The Art of Innovation*.[14] The team was tasked to take an existing shopping cart and redesign it. Part of their design process involved exploring the problem from multiple perspectives. An interdisciplinary team made up of people with diverse expertise that ranged from a biologist to a psychologist participated in this process.

They interviewed people who use and repair shopping carts to see what they thought about the cart. They looked at data such as the number of child injuries and theft. They went to a grocery store to observe how people used the shopping carts. They studied the situation from multiple perspectives. By carefully observing things that most people typically do not notice, they came up with a newly redesigned shopping cart that separated the groceries out into sections so that the meats and the vegetables were separated.

The point here is that observation and multiple perspectives are necessary components to figuring out an interesting challenge or problem for a project. Dr. Barufaldi explained why he engaged in challenging projects:

> I think they are fun for one thing. I think working within and outside of the (education) system is fascinating. I think I thrive on challenge. That is synergy!

The following interviews reveal how these successful leaders identified challenging problems. The bulleted points are strategies that you can use to find interesting problems to solve.

> ➤ *Be open to new ideas by collaborating with people.*

Collaboration allows you to see and get different perspectives on situations and things and bounce around ideas with others. It also makes visible what you may not typically notice. Ideas might be sparked to frame situations or problems in different ways through collaboration. Dr. James Barufaldi stated:

> I think that is something I get from listening to people, from collaborating, from traveling. "What am I going to do next?" I always have a project in mind. When I don't, I think I am going to die [laughs]. I always have an idea to pursue. I don't know. Maybe that is part of my personality. I am not too sure. That is synergy behind what I do.

➢ *Listen and pay attention to community needs.*

The leaders interviewed paid attention to the needs of the community they serve. They observed things from their community perspective. They listened to multiple perspectives. They spent time watching and understanding. They studied up on topics. They also simultaneously thought about how to get "buy-in" and support from their stakeholders.

It is a two-way interaction, as opposed to researchers being all-knowing experts who are going to tell people what they are doing right or wrong. For example, Dr. Richard Milner said that he made sure that he listened to people's perspectives from all walks of life. He explained:

> I try to listen to people from varied background and disciplinary expertise and also people from outside of academia. I am deliberate about taking advice from people from varied walks of life. I am not an elitist. I have learned from blue-collar workers, at the supermarket. I am drawn to the human spirit.

In considering the needs of the community you serve, you must pay attention. What is the real issue or problem? Having different perspectives of others who can identify and define the problem is helpful.

➢ *Get some background information through reading.*

Knowlege is an important part of creativity and the creative process. To bend the rules, an individual needs to know the rules first. In order to be creative or come up with a novel idea, a sound knowledge base is needed to make connections and make informed decisions. Dr. Barufaldi shared that he reads and studies a lot before he embarks on a project:

> In my situation, I do a lot of reading. I do some research on the basic core ideas. I think it is about listening to people in what their needs and concerns are. You know like now in Texas, I think one of the most immediate needs and concerns right now is to look over the relationship between poverty and education. . . . I think it is focusing on the needs and concerns of individuals within the community. I was good at always picking up on those needs and concerns. We do a lot of surveys and interviews to find out what those needs are. I have always tapped into surveys, telephone calls, and interviews before starting any project.

➢ *Be curious; ask interesting questions.*

Asking the right questions and being curious can lead to exciting projects. Dr. Mitchell Nathan shared an example of the kind of questions he asked about things that interested him. These questions resulted in interesting projects. He shared that most of his questions came from trying to make sense of something. Sometimes it involves looking at perspectives from an interdisciplinary lens. Anyone can ask interesting questions from an interdisciplinary lens. The important point is that asking questions and being curious is an important part of innovating.

Dr. Mitchell Nathan has an impressive résumé. He is currently a professor of learning science at the University of Wisconsin at Madison. He is the director of the Center for Education and Work and the Institute of Educational Sciences (IES) Post-Doctoral Fellowship Program in Mathematical Thinking, Learning, and Instruction. Some of his affiliations include the National Academy of Science, the National Research Council, and Board of Science Education. He is also affiliated with the National Academy of Engineering Committee on Integrated STEM Education. Dr. Nathan stated:

> I do recall at some point in college when I first learned about artificial intelligence and robotics thinking, like this is one of the most exciting things out there and I want to devote my intellectual energy. I wanted to understand *"What that was about?"* because it sounded so profound and, I guess, part of the appeal was that I was studying computer science and engineering. . . .
>
> But I was also very interested in the humanities and social sciences at this time. I did a double major originally with engineering and history because I had both sides of my intellectual curiosity in both those realms. I got pulled in early as a fellow in the engineering and public policy center at Carnegie Mellon.[15]

One of the key things to notice is that his love and curiosity led him to pursue things. He examined things from an interdisciplinary perspective:

> I was working with Robert Ayres and Steven Miller, who was interested in the social implications of robotics. Prof. Ayres wanted someone who would not be overwhelmed by the technical details of the robotic systems that would be written about; . . . we did this with another fellow, Steven Miller. We traveled to some of these factories and stuff where they were considered exemplary uses of early robotic systems like auto manufacturing and milling type of products in Milwaukee and other cities. So, the question is pretty cool, *"What are the social implications of robotics?"* It was the first time I started to realize that people can do research on social science. . . .
>
> I was more familiar with engineering and the hard sciences that hypothesize about the natural world, and you certainly read classic experiments that scientists had done about the speed of light. In engineering, so-called research was like building something. You try to innovate and build something new. And I was at the time not as familiar with this side of engineering but did research on the human factors and more of a social sciences side. But there is absolutely a technical side of it. So that opened up my eyes that one could do research and have a career in research and have questions not only about the natural world but obviously artificial intelligence and robotics.

Dr. Nathan worked with people who did interesting things. He traveled to factories to get a "hands-on" real-world context to explore how things work. His journey involved an exploration of different disciplines, working with people he found interesting and exploring real-world settings. He went to work on robotics research and development, building autonomous vehicles that could drive on roads without a person, using computer vision and artificial intelligence (AI).

> They hinge on the questions about the human situation and *"What does it mean to perceive something and "What does it mean to know and experience something?"* So they were never in my upbringing framed as computational questions or mathematical questions or engineering questions. They were always straddling that side of human experience with the science and the math.

Dr. Nathan's thinking process emerged out of his curiosity and experiences as he wondered about things. This type of questioning is what drove his research agenda. It also shows the importance of connecting things from two different fields and how it can lead to asking profound questions. This was just part of the work he did. Dr. Nathan's curiosity and exploration of ideas led to questions that he explored as part of his research.

> ➤ *Connecting things from an interdisciplinary perspective might lead to profound questions.*

Being curious and asking questions should not just be limited to academics. Anyone can ask interesting questions and wonder about things. The key is to not limit questioning to one perspective. Sometimes thinking about a problem from an interdisciplinary perspective might be helpful. For example, a teacher could ask questions as to why students have difficulty grasping a concept. Was the task appropriate? Did students have the background knowledge? Were the materials used appropriately?

A grade-level team could explore teaching lessons, look at student work, and wonder about what sense the students were making. A principal could ask questions and wonder about better ways to support students and teachers from an interdisciplinary lens.

> ➤ *Be open to possibilities in an organic way.*

Dr. Rochelle Gutiérrez pointed out that she does not have a predetermined path but is open to opportunities and things that arise naturally. She finds interesting problems to solve based on the needs of the community that she is serving and things that she notices. Effective leaders think long term. They think about how today's action will lead to future work. Dr. Gutiérrez stated:

A lot of my work is very organic. I try to be responsive to the situation and to the people in it. I don't start out thinking I know exactly what I am going to do. I have a direction but not a destination.

Strategies for Finding Interesting Problems to Solve

Think about a challenge that you are encountering in your work setting. Think about the problem from multiple perspectives. Part of this process is defining the problem before you can come up with a creative solution.

> ➤ Be open to new ideas by listening and collaborating with people.
> ➤ Listen and pay attention to community needs.
> ➤ Read/research to get some background information.
> ➤ Be curious. Ask interesting questions.
> ➤ Be open to possibilities in an organic way.

ARTICULATE VISION INTO ACTION

Now that you have dreamed your dream, what is your vision? What are you trying to accomplish? What problem are you going to solve? What does your dream pragmatically look like? How do you build a bridge between your vision and moving forward? This part involves getting focused and thinking outside the box. Anthony Robbins, author of *Unlimited Power*, states that to achieve success, a vision must be defined, challenging goals must be set, and a plan of action needs to be created.[16]

Once you have figured out what you want to accomplish, then you must develop an action plan to put your vision into motion. Steve Covey, the author of *The 7 Habits of Highly Effective People*, points out that one of the things that successful people do is think about what they want to accomplish first before embarking on a journey.[17] My interview with Dr. Barufaldi revealed how he put his vision into action:

You must keep that end goal in mind. You must have a plan or mental plan. How do you get from point A to point B? Where do you get the resources? Who are you going to work with? Where do you get the money? Everyone in Texas believed in what I was doing. If I was going to do something outlandish, I would not have lasted in this place. All my ideas were consistent with the Board of Regents, consistent with our president, our dean, and department chair. . . .

It should be aligned with the mission of the organization. I always made sure that I was consistent with the tenants. If you don't have that alignment, your long-term goal will not be achieved. You will have too many stumbling blocks in the way.

An interesting point that Dr. Barufaldi made was that aligning your work with the mission of the institution/context that you are working with is necessary for success. Also, thinking through issues and having a plan of action helps.

Develop an Action Plan

Action Items

> ➢ Come up with a plan to accomplish goals.
> ➢ Be specific—what do you want to accomplish?
> ➢ What steps are you going to take?
> ➢ What tools and resources do you need?
> ➢ How are you going to manage time?
> ➢ Who do you need on your team?

CHAPTER SUMMARY

Find your higher purpose, and figure out your action plan. Finding your higher purpose motivates you to act.

A leader who leads a team to innovate is someone who can lead a team to learn and think creatively to innovate. The goal is to make things better for others. This is different than a manager who just keeps things running.

A great leader is an individual driven by passion fueled by his or her higher purpose. The leader's journey is shaped by his or her life story, which inspires a sensitivity to make a difference. Blind optimism inspires the journey because the leader believes that anything is possible. The leader "walks the walk and talks the talk." In other words, the leader's actions are authentic. Imagination and visualization of the possibilities inspire the leader to dream of something others might not consider realistic or even feasible.

The great leader is aware and pays attention to the community that he or she serves. This makes the leader a lifelong learner who has a thirst for adventure and new knowledge. The leader has a curious mind that allows extraordinary things to happen where innovation can take place. The leader's vision is the initial spark to lead a team. Once the leader assembles a team, then a vision is co-created, and action is taken to drive the team to innovate and do extraordinary things.

STRATEGIES FOR BUILDING AN ACTION PLAN

Identify Your Interests, Passions, and Core Values to Define Your Agenda

- Identify what you are passionate about and what you stand for. Find your higher purpose.
- Identify your core values.
- Align your actions with your core values and passions.
- Visualize the possibilities of what you can achieve over time.
- Find interesting challenges to solve.

Journal

Write down your interests, and narrow your focus. Identify what areas you want to concentrate on over time to develop expertise.

How to Identify Interesting and Meaningful Problems to Solve

- Be open to new ideas by collaborating with people.
- Listen and pay attention to community needs.
- Read to get some background information.
- Be curious. Ask interesting questions.
- Be open to possibilities in an organic way.

Develop an Action Plan

- Be specific: What do you want to accomplish?
- What steps are you going to take?
- What tools and resources do you need?
- How are you going to manage time?
- Who do you need on your team?

NOTES

1. Dr. Richard Milner, interview by Teruni Lamberg. All quotations of Dr. Milner in this book are from this interview.
2. Dr. Rochelle Gutiérrez, interview by Teruni Lamberg. All quotations of Dr. Gutiérrez in this book are from this interview.
3. John Maxwell, *21 Irrefutable Laws of Leadership: Follow Them and People Will Follow You* (Nashville, TN: Thomas Nelson, 2007).
4. John P. Kotter, *Leading Change* (Boston: Harvard Business Review Press, 2012).

5. Jack Canfield and Janet Switzer, *The Success Principles: How to Get from Where You Are to Where You Want to Be* (New York: HarperCollins, 2005).

6. Bill George, *Discover Your True North: Become an Authentic Leader*, 2nd ed. (Holbrook, NJ: John Wiley and Sons, 2015).

7. George, *Discover Your True North*.

8. James Kouzes and Barry Posner, *Leadership Challenge: How to Make Extraordinary Things Happen in Organizations*, 5th ed. (San Francisco: Jossey-Bass, 2012); George, *Discover Your True North*.

9. Sibyl Kaufman, "STEM Teaching: Retiring Not Retiring," *University of Texas Education Magazine*, August 2005.

10. Kouzes and Posner, *Leadership Challenge*.

11. George, *Discover Your True North*.

12. Kouzes and Posner, *Leadership Challenge*.

13. Dan Rather, "ABC Nightline—IDEO Shopping Cart," *YouTube*, published December 2, 2009, by Alfonso Neri, www.youtube.com/watch?v=M66ZU2PCIcM.

14. Tom Kelly, *The Art of Innovation: Lessons in Creativity from IDEO America's Leading Design Firm* (New York: Doubleday, 2007).

15. Dr. Mitchell Nathan, interview by Teruni Lamberg. All quotations of Dr. Nathan in this book are from this interview.

16. Anthony Robbins, *Unlimited Power: The New Science of Personal Achievement* (New York: Simon and Schuster, 2015).

17. Steve Covey, *The 7 Habits of Highly Effective People* (New York: Free Press, 2014).

Two

How to Assemble an Interdisciplinary Team to Solve a Problem

In the long history of humankind those who learned to collaborate and improvise most effectively have prevailed.

—Charles Darwin

Selecting team members that work well together is vital for a successful project. *The right combination of team members can make extraordinary things happen.* The team must function synergistically together to spark innovative ideas. This chapter explores how to conceptualize the kind of expertise that is needed to solve a problem. Selecting team members requires careful thought.

Think About . . .

➢ What leadership experiences have you had? What worked or did not work?

➢ How can you draw from these experiences to help you lead teams to do innovative things?

VISUALIZE A PROBLEM FROM A 360-DEGREE PERSPECTIVE TO SELECT YOUR TEAM

The world is but a canvas to our imagination.

—Henry David Thoreau

Visualizing a problem from multiple perspectives is helpful to explore the kind of expertise needed to solve a problem. For example, Dr. Mitchell Nathan looked at things from a 360-degree viewpoint. He explained that when you conduct research in education, you need to think about *learning* from multiple perspectives. Therefore, he carefully thought about the expertise needed and who to invite to be part of his team.

He did this by thinking about the *parts* and *pieces* needed to solve the problem. He gave an example of how he put a team together to figure out how to support students learning algebra by exploring how algebraic thinking develops. This is an important topic because algebra is a gatekeeper for many students to pursue many career paths in math, science, and engineering. Therefore, there is a need to help students be successful math students by learning algebra so that it makes sense to them. It was important to understand how to help kids learn algebra.

Dr. Nathan coauthored with Karen Koellner a paper titled *A Framework for Understanding and Cultivating the Transition from Arithmetic to Algebraic Reasoning.*[1] This article lays out a conceptual framework for the kind of thinking needed for the development of algebraic reasoning and the learning and teaching processes involved. Specifically, the model integrates three dimensions: (1) student learning and development; (2) teacher knowledge, beliefs, and practices; and (3) teacher professional development.

First, he thought about how people learn algebra through an interdisciplinary lens. He wanted to explore how to support students to transition from arithmetic thinking practices to algebraic practices. This process might involve students coming up with their own solution methods and representations. The goal was to understand how to support students to learn algebra so that it was meaningful and made sense. Dr. Nathan explored this problem from a holistic point of view:

> I realized that you needed to understand the developmental level of algebraic thinking. You needed to understand the cognitive psychology part of algebraic thinking. You needed to understand teacher professional development. You should understand curriculum design and how standards and curricula are used in teaching practice. . . .
>
>   You should understand assessment practices and how assessments define what someone else says they know or have learned. I know that there are all those parts. And that is where assembling a team came about. I wanted to pursue this question.

The important part to note is that the question of "How does an understanding of the ways that algebraic reasoning develops serve as a foundation to support the teaching and learning of algebra?" influenced Dr. Nathan's thinking.

➢ *Examine parts and pieces and the big picture to determine team expertise.*

People with expertise and mutual interest were identified and recruited. The mind map in figure 2.1 illustrates Dr. Nathan's thinking.

I thought it could only be done in a large team with some experts in every one of those areas that I just said. So, I went and found people and put a team together that represented all the puzzle pieces (to solve the problem). We all had a *common vision. The common vision is what we now call a 360-degree view.* . . .

We did not have that phrase then, you know; we had a view of all these parts and pieces that we knew would come together, because there is *no way to change the system or fully understand the system* just by only looking at one of these. We had to look at all of them.

The lens that Dr. Nathan took was a 360-degree view of solving the problem. He considered how the parts and pieces tied to solving the problem.

Not only did he think about the kind of experts he needed, but he also thought about how to get the resources he needed. He wrote a grant and got funded for six years to work with a large research team across several universities:

> We wrote a large grant for that. We did get that. That was a joint venture with National Science Foundation, U.S. Department of Education, and NIH. They all put their money into this program called the IERI,[2] and that was great because it ended up being a six-year grant with seven co-principal investigators.

Think about what you are trying to accomplish. What problem are you trying to solve? Dr. Craig Wall, who was part of the Nevada Mathematics Project, pointed out that this was an important question to consider before finding a solution.

Write down a problem that you are trying to solve, and make a sketch of the parts and pieces involved in solving the problem. You don't have to be a researcher to think this way. Perhaps you might be part of a church group trying to make a difference. You may be part of a nonprofit organization seeking to come up with innovative ways to help people.

Perhaps you are a principal, curriculum coordinator, or teacher leader trying to solve a problem. When you think about the "big picture" and the parts involved, it allows you to figure out what (people, resources, and actions) you need to solve your problem. Think creatively. What kind of expertise is required to address the problem that you identified?

Think About . . .

> ➢ What problem are you trying to solve?
> ➢ What are the parts and pieces?
> ➢ What kind of skills, expertise, and talent are needed to accomplish the task?
> ➢ Create your own mind map of the problem situation and the expertise needed to solve the problem.

> ➤ *When meeting people with interesting ideas and passion, be open to possibilities of collaboration.*

A team may emerge when a passionate group of individuals with a common goal has a spark to work together.

Case Study: Nevada Mathematics Project

When I was writing the grant proposal for the Nevada Mathematics Project, I thought about who I wanted on my team. As I mentioned before, I had put a statewide effort together that involved multi-institutional collaborations. The first two years of our project focused on math.

> ➤ *Identify a problem, let ideas simmer, and be open to possibilities.*

The third year, I knew that I needed something extra to keep my team excited and motivated to participate. This project had demanded a lot from my team. We had traveled together for the past two years and conducted workshops for four weeks in the summer and fifteen follow-up sessions during the school year around the state of Nevada.

This pretty much required giving up weekends and even bringing our families during parts of the project on the road. It involved driving over 19,000 miles!

The teachers had been with us for the previous two years as well. We needed to figure out a way to keep them excited to participate in the project in the third year.

A new edge or perspective to generate a spark of renewed interest was necessary. We did not want our third year to be simply a routine event where we just went through the motions of professional development.

> ➤ *Incubation of ideas is essential to generate new ones.*

The problem described above was simmering in my head, but I had not come up with a solution. I was unsure which direction to take. An unexpected sequence of events took place. *Sometimes, the most unexpected things happen that provide opportunities to spark new and innovative ideas.* When this happens, you must be open to new possibilities and seize them as opportunities to be creative.

> ➤ *The important part is to pay attention to people and ideas!*

There was a mathematics education conference held in East Lansing, Michigan. I was living in Reno and needed to figure out how to get from Detroit to East Lansing. I was a little nervous about traveling from the Detroit airport to East Lansing in the winter. I had visions of getting stuck in the snow. (Even though, as I learned later, Reno got more snow than Detroit during that time.)

It so happened that a dear friend named Dr. Craig Wall (who I knew as a nineteen-year-old college student at the University of Texas at Austin) had moved to Detroit. We had not seen each other for many years. Our life paths took us in different directions. We had reconnected on LinkedIn. He was gracious enough to offer me a ride from the Detroit airport to East Lansing. I had no idea of distance, and it turned out to be a two-hour car ride! I had not seen him for several years, so it gave us an opportunity to catch up.

I learned that he had pursued his doctorate in chemistry and was working in the field of nanotechnology. During our car ride, I joked that I was now doing STEM at my institution and perhaps we should collaborate. This joke turned into an idea. When I initially joked, it seemed such a far-fetched idea. How in the world would nanotechnology have anything to do with K–8 education?

That very same weekend, I joined a group of scholars at the conference that evening to socialize. It was at this moment that I met Dr. Mitchell Nathan. I learned that he worked with Dr. John Bransford at the Cognition and Technology Group. I was delighted to know that he too had done a postdoctorate at Vanderbilt and was part of the Cognition and Technology Group. I then learned that he was researching how people use gestures to enhance meaning and learning. He studies how teachers use gestures to communicate and help students make meaning. We chatted about the possibility of collaborating. It was a delightful evening.

> *Engage in creative thinking by connecting ideas and people to create a spark for collaboration!*
> *Thinking about connections between ideas is helpful for coming up with creative solutions.*

For example, when I returned to Reno, and the ideas encountered when traveling to the conference were simmering in my head. I knew the new grant proposals would be coming out soon. The call for proposals announcement for the grant funding arrived a couple of days later in my email inbox.

This time, the state vision for funding was integrated STEM statewide. This made me think about the original idea of context. Implementing professional development with random math problems that did not connect to each other and topics seemed kind of boring. As I mentioned before, the third year we needed a spark to keep the project going. I needed to think creatively.

Creative thinking does not occur in a vacuum. John Eric Adiar, who wrote the book *The Art of Creative Thinking: How to be Innovative and Develop Great Ideas*, points out that our environment contains everything a person needs to think with such as things, people, and ideas. Adiar points out that *a creative person can see connections among things or ideas in novel ways with what already exists.*[3] For example, the ability to see the connection of using nanotechnology as a context for teaching data analysis and geometry involves creative thought.

The important take away from this experience is to think about a problem that you want to solve and let your ideas simmer. When opportunities, ideas, and resources present themselves, be open to possibilities of making novel connections. Imagination is the first step to thinking about a possibility without constraints, and feasibility can be decided later.

The bottom line is that ideas take time to germinate. Many times, if we try to force ideas out of nothing, we may encounter writer's block or a lack of ideas. *The act of immersing yourself in ideas and continually reflecting on it consciously and unconsciously will lead to awareness when opportunities present themselves.* This process helped me think about the third phase of the Nevada Mathematics Project.

> ➢ *Actively think about the problem and explore ideas to make connections to come up with a plan.*

Thinking about the problem, drawing on prior experiences and knowledge, and seeking connections can lead to a solution.

Case Study: Nevada Mathematics Project

The purpose of the Nevada Math Project was to support teachers to teach the Nevada Academic Content Standards based on the Common Core. We had explored two-thirds of the standards in the previous institutes. Data analysis, statistics, and geometry still needed to be addressed. A unique context was needed to tie data analysis, statistics, and geometry as topics for professional development so that there was coherence and meaning. In addition, I needed to think about ways to make this institute interesting so that teachers would be excited to learn something new.

My post-doctoral work with Dr. Paul Cobb involved working on a research project that included helping teachers improve their understanding of data analysis and statistics. Therefore, I had some ideas about how to help teachers to learn this topic. I then needed to think about how the subject of geometry could work with data analysis and statistics for the teacher institutes we were planning on doing.

My earlier research had involved thinking a lot about how to motivate students to learn. At that time, I was learning about project-based learning as a vehicle to motivate students. This is when you use real-world problems for students to solve and come up with a solution. I was inspired by Dr. John Bransford's work from the Cognition and Technology Group at Vanderbilt University. Dr. Nathan was part of that group. My doctoral dissertation built on his ideas. I developed an Anchored instruction video inspired by their work.

Dr. Craig Wall had sent me a couple of books to read on nanotechnology. This was not a topic that I was an expert in. As I started reading them, I began to realize that Northwestern had done a lot of work in this area in making scientific discoveries. The idea emerged in my head about the possibility of combining nanotechnology with data analysis and geometry.

I searched the internet to see if any teaching materials were available on this topic. I wanted to know if this idea was feasible. To my surprise, I discovered Northwestern had developed modules about nanotechnology for K–12 students. Furthermore, it was aligned to the Next Generation Science Standards and the Common Core mathematics standards.

> ➤ *Actively explore ideas to determine feasibility, and be willing to think outside your comfort zone.*

Innovation involves coming up with novel ideas. Part of innovating involves taking risks.

Case Study: Nevada Mathematics Project, Continued

Therefore, to pursue the idea of combining nanotechnology with the math, the feasibility of the idea needed to be explored. So I contacted the Northwestern Materials Research Center. Professor Chang, the center director of materials research, answered the phone.

He shared with me that his Center for Materials Research had invested millions of dollars in developing innovative materials to help K–12 students understand nanotechnology and math. He wanted to share these Northwestern Materials Worlds Modules with teachers and students.

He put me in touch with Dr. Mathew Hsu, who was instrumental in developing the modules. The Nanotechnology Modules provided a context to integrate the topics of data analysis and geometry. The possibility of combining mathematics with nanotechnology to help teachers develop and increase their content and pedagogical knowledge then became a reality.

> ➤ *Getting support from teammates is essential for coming up with innovative solutions.*

Getting the support of the team is essential for taking on a new project and solving problems.

Case Study: Nevada Mathematics Project

Therefore, the existing project team members brainstormed about the possibility of including and expanding on the research gestures and nanotechnology as part of the project. The Nevada Mathematics Project team loved the idea of having the context of science to wrap around the math.

They also liked the idea of integrating the research on gestures to support teacher learning because the process of teaching and learning was an explicit goal of the project. They thought that it would be brilliant. So I contacted Dr.

Nathan and asked what he thought about working with us on the project and embedding the research on gestures to support teacher learning.

Dr. Steven Damelin, a mathematician who works at Mathematical Reviews, also joined the team. He had a curiosity and interest in using concept maps to teach mathematics. Also, Dr. Diana Moss from Appalachian State and Dr. Rebecca Boncoddo, a cognitive psychologist from Central Connecticut University, joined our team as well to collaborate on research on gestures and integrate a cognitive psychology perspective. The dynamics of social interaction are an important part to consider when selecting the team along with the expertise.

> ➤ *Connect parts to the "big picture."*
> ➤ *Novelty adds excitement!*

We decided to use nanotechnology as a context for teaching mathematics through science. We decided to embed the research and conduct additional research on gestures. The research team was made up of scientists, mathematicians, math educators, cognitive scientists, school district leaders, and regional trainers.

This team came together because it involved making connections between ideas, people, and events. The diagram in figure 2.1 represents the mind map of the Nevada Mathematics Project and how ideas and people were connected to form the project team.

The expertise map in figure 2.1 represents an interdisciplinary perspective and a synthesis of the parts and pieces needed to explore a problem.

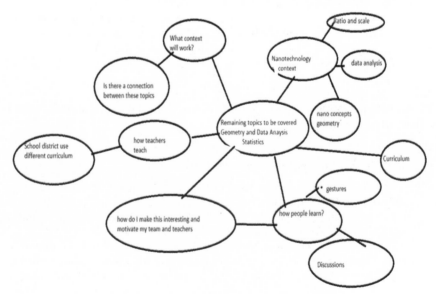

Figure 2.1. Expertise Map of the Nevada Mathematics Project Team
Credit: Teruni Lamberg.

Dr. Howard Gardner wrote an article about the "five minds for the future." He viewed the future as being made up of an interconnected world of science, technology, economy, and society. He described the kinds of minds needed for the future. The ability to have interdisciplinary minds and synthesize information will be powerful for the future. Particularly, he pointed out that the mind should be able to make sense of multiple sources of information and decide what is important and put the information together in a way that makes sense to self and others.[4]

> ➤ *The possibility for collaboration exists if individuals have an interest or a motive to participate.*

People need a reason to help solve a problem even though they might have the right background. There is a human and intellectual dimension for people to join. Most people are willing to participate if they can get something from experience and have something to contribute.

Case Study: Nevada Mathematics Project

Dr. Craig Wall wanted to join our work with me due to our friendship and because he felt that students needed to understand science from an interdisciplinary perspective. He explained that he felt a strong desire to make a difference in the lives of children.

Dr. Mitchell Nathan wanted to be able to take the research that he was doing and share it with teachers. Dr. Chang had developed very high-quality nanotechnology modules and was trying to figure out a way to share this with schools. Ms. Peggy Lakey, Dr. Travis Olson, and Dr. Edward Keppelman cared deeply about helping Nevada teachers and students.

Dr. Steven Damelin was very interested in mathematics, concept maps, and how children learn. There was a spark or passion in everyone to participate. Everyone was also motivated by the higher purpose of making a difference.

> ➤ *A common purpose brings people together.*

When people with shared passion/interest get together around a common goal, they can become a community of practice that generates knowledge. Wenger and Snyder called this shared purpose a "joint enterprise." Etienne Wenger and William Snyder wrote an article in the *Harvard Business Review* on how a community of practice functions. Basically, how people interact with each other influences the knowledge that gets generated.[5]

The Nevada Math Project team came together because the team members wanted to learn from each other and help teachers become better math and science teachers. Wenger and Snyder point out that when *people get together with a shared purpose, it typically involves forming cross-functional teams and not necessary organizational teams.* Wenger and Snyder write that the primary goal of a community of practice is to develop and exchange knowledge. The glue that holds the group together is passion, commitment, and identification with the group expertise. They make a distinction between a community of practice and a project team. They point out that in a project team, people are assigned tasks and held together with project milestones and goals until the project is completed.[6]

Case Study: Nevada Mathematics Project

The Nevada Mathematics Project became a community of practice, and the glue that held people together was passion. Once the project was formalized, it became a project team that had milestones to be accomplished. Passion was instrumental for the motivation of the team and their ability to innovate.

The interactions shifted between being a project team trying to accomplish things to a community of practice that generated knowledge. The next chapter will explore this interaction. The third year, the integration of nanotechnology, math, and research on gestures added novelty to the project. The new team members rejuvenated the excitement of the project. Innovation helps to keep a team motivated and interested in exploring and trying new things. Having interesting people join the team can add value as well.

Think About . . .

> ➤ What problem are you trying to solve?
> ➤ What are the parts and pieces?
> ➤ Let your mind think about this over time.
> ➤ Think about the problem, or redefine the problem.
> ➤ Be open to ideas as you travel to new places, meet new people, and let your ideas germinate.
> ➤ Be mindful of new opportunities, interactions with people, and resources that can lead to new possibilities.
> ➤ When putting a team together, articulate joint enterprise.
> ➤ Combine the idea of a community of practice with a project team to be innovative. (A community of practice is when people get together based on a common purpose to generate ideas.)

CHOOSE TEAM MEMBERS THAT SHARE PASSION AND A COMMON PURPOSE

Carefully choosing team members is important. Diverse expertise and background add value to a team. It allows the team to explore a problem and come up with a creative solution from multiple perspectives. When a higher purpose motivates team members, they are more likely to be motivated to contribute and be willing to go the distance to make the project a success.

Ideally, the team members must be willing to work toward a common purpose and be able to function together as a team. Bill George points out the importance of having a diverse team. He suggests that a leader should surround themselves with people whose strengths complement their weaknesses.[7]

If a team member's vision or purpose is not aligned with the goals of the project, then that person may not be a good fit. Therefore, carefully selecting the team members is important. Consider the following points when choosing team members.

> ➢ *Read people; listen to your gut instinct to see if a potential team member is a good fit.*

Dr. Barufaldi shared that it was crucial to select the right people. He explained that choosing the right people can be cumbersome and very time-consuming and that once a team clicks together, individuals who don't fit leave the team. He would then end up inviting new members. One of the interesting things he pointed out when selecting people was his ability to read people intuitively:

> A good leader must be able to read people. Some people don't have that knack or ability. I can read people within three seconds. . . . If you can really work with that person, or not work with that person. There is something in that initial interaction. At the same time you should give everyone the opportunity to become part of that collaborative if you wish to do that. To make them feel part of the ownership. . . .
>
> People have told me that I am a very good reader of people. All throughout my career, even when I was a high school supervisor, department chair in science, I could separate those teachers who I could really read quickly and those that I knew that I had a difficult time [reading].

Daniel Goleman coauthored a book titled *Primal Leadership*. In this book, he points out that effective leaders have high emotional intelligence.[8] They are self- and socially aware and can build teams by paying attention to people's emotions and being able to respond to people. Dr. Barufaldi explained what he looked for in people:

> It is knowing that you can work with this person. It is not just about sharing similar views or points of view. It is just that you know that that person has a certain degree of openness that you can tap into, and a leader must have the same qualities also. It is about reading the individual. . . .

Maybe it is eye contact, the way they present themselves; you also know if it is an egotistical person and it is about me, me, and me. . . . You know that right away. I know that I won't want to work with that person right away. That person is outgoing, warm, understanding, sensitive, and you know about that person within the first five minutes.

He made it clear to me that it is important for a leader to realize that it is not their project. "It is everyone's project. It is everyone's goal to achieve."

SELECT TEAM MEMBERS WHO
WORK SYNERGISTICALLY TOGETHER

A well-functioning team works synergistically together. This means that each person makes a unique contribution and works together toward a common goal. The glue that holds the team together is a common purpose and passion. When everyone is working toward the common purpose, great things can happen.

Many of the leaders interviewed pointed out that the character of the team members matters. These characteristics include your ability to trust that person, the person's beliefs and convictions being aligned with the project, and the person having integrity and the right attitude. These are essential qualities to produce extraordinary results. When these qualities are lacking in a team member, that person can derail the team.[9]

Team members must function as a team and have specific roles. However, the roles and how the team functions should be flexible. Dr. Paul Cobb shared that he thinks about building a research team as analogous to assembling a sports team. He called it a "gap-closing process." He explained that you select people to play different roles in the project like a baseball team. However, he also pointed out that these roles are not that rigid. There is flexibility on how the team functions. Dr. Cobb stated:

Yes, you do have some ideas of certain people's capabilities. . . . What I am also trying to say is that you also try to adapt the project to the people. You also adapt the work to the people. So that is what I mean when I say, "gap closing."

Dr. Richard Milner also shared how he thought about how the team members may contribute to the project:

I asked myself, "Who shares a similar interest in this space? What might they be able to contribute collaboratively and individually? How might this project advance their own knowledge and career and their narrative, and what might their work life be?"

> *Select team members to play different roles within the project.*

Think About . . .

> ➢ You have already selected your team members based on the expertise you need.
> ➢ Think about each team member's role in the project.
> ➢ Be flexible with project goals so that the project adapts to expertise and interest.

CHARACTER MATTERS

> ➢ *Pick team members whom you can trust.*

Expertise and experience alone are not enough. You need people who you can work with. Dr. Richard Milner shared how he put a team together. He picked team members who had varying levels of expertise. One of the most important qualities he looked for was *trust*:

> I spend a lot of time thinking about the varying expertise that people bring, the different experience levels that people have, and a very important element is trust. Because I cannot work with people who I cannot trust. The human and heart element is important. The relationship piece for effectiveness as team members. . . .
>
> It would be difficult to me to work with someone who I did not trust even if the person is brilliant. I put teams together based on trust and diversity of perspectives based on my history with people.

Kouzes and Posner point out that trust is an essential ingredient of collaboration.[10] Therefore, selecting people that you can trust is a major step toward building a team whose members will share ideas with each other and collaborate so that they can innovate. Others such as Dr. Jbeily shared this view.

I met Dr. Kamil Jbeily many years ago at the U.S. Department of Education annual meeting. Dr. Jbeily shared with me the work he was doing in Texas. He had founded and directed the Texas Regional Collaboratives for Excellence in Science and Mathematics Program at the University of Texas at Austin. This program was highly successful and has won many awards over the years.

Texas is a geographically vast state made up of cities with dense populations along with rural areas. I was privileged to attend an impressive "Honoring the Teachers" ceremony and an "Annual Meeting" event sponsored by the Texas Regional Collaboratives, where I got to witness Texas educators and stakeholders come together to celebrate the year's accomplishments.

This work inspired my work in Nevada. It helped me conceptualize how to organize a statewide effort. Dr. Jbeily has incredible leadership skills to have pulled off such an impressive effort across Texas. Interviewing him was a privilege. Dr. Jbeily's passion, his genuine love of people, and his selfless desire to help others and make a difference became apparent.

> ➢ *Select individuals with a healthy attitude!*
> ➢ *Every success begins with a healthy attitude!*

Dr. Jbeily shared his thoughts about attributes to consider when selecting team members:

> Every success begins with a healthy attitude. People who really apply what they know, act on what they know, and believe in the application of the information. People who are pragmatic and want results. I emphasize the word *attitude* because it is so hard to change people's attitude.[11]

Dr. Jbeily stressed that it is important to select team members with the right attitude. He emphasized how important attitude was when he hired people to work with him or selected team members. He gained the following insight when flying Southwest Airlines (SWA) as a frequent flyer customer. He noticed that the employees seemed happy and had a positive attitude.

He was curious about this. So he asked the flight attendants, pilots, and other SWA employees why this was the case. "Why are the employees so happy and cheerful?" One lead flight attendant had to think about this for a while. In the middle of the flight, she came back to him and said that she had an explanation. She had worked the human resources at SWA. She explained to Dr. Jbeily the following:

> At SWA, prospective employees are subjected to the following litmus test: "SWA hires for attitude and trains for knowledge and skills. If the person's attitude is rotten, he or she is not hired regardless of qualifications."[22]

> ➢ *Select members who have strong convictions, not just beliefs.*

You need people who have strong convictions. For example, in the Nevada Mathematics Project, team members have been chosen based on their strong desire to help teachers learn so that they can support their students. Dr. Jbeily emphasized that you need people with strong convictions. These are committed individuals who are willing to go the distance to contribute and make the project a success. According to Dr. Jbeily:

> You want a person who has convictions, not just beliefs. The person with conviction is ready to stand out on a limb because he firmly believes that limb is going to grow into a large branch that will provide the shade from the hot Texas sun! You are willing to stand out on a limb. That's conviction!

Think About . . .

> ➤ What expertise and perspective will the team member bring to the team?
> ➤ Why would this individual want to participate?
> ➤ What is this individual's motivation for participating?
> ➤ How would this person fit with the rest of the team?

SUPPORT TEAM MEMBERS PERSONAL ASPIRATIONS

The bottom line is that people have many demands on their time and for the most part they are busy. If this is the case, why would they want to be on your team? What is in it for them? This is an important consideration when selecting team members. An effective leader cares about the team and the well-being of each team member.

Be a servant leader who cares about the mission and the team. Therefore, it is important to consider why someone would like to participate in your team. What benefit would they get out of it? The other part is how that person can justify their time to the division or institution that this is a worthwhile cause. Each member should get some benefit for contributing and being part of the team. This will lead to greater motivation to participate.

Think About . . .

> ➤ When selecting team members:
> ➤ Read people; listen to your gut instinct to see if a potential team member is a good fit.
> ➤ Select team members to play different roles within the project.
> ➤ Pick team members that you can trust.
> ➤ Select people with a healthy attitude!
> ➤ Select members who have strong convictions, not just beliefs.
> ➤ Think about how to support personal aspirations of team members.

CHAPTER SUMMARY

Develop a strategic vision and assemble a dream team.
Defining your vision allows you to select your team members strategically.

The leader needs to visualize what he or she is trying to accomplish from a 360-degree perspective to decide what kind of expertise is required in the team. The leader should carefully select team members so that their interests and passions are aligned. The bottom line is that people have many demands on their time, and for the most part they are busy. If this is the case, think about why they would want to be on your team. What is in it for them?

Consider the kind of expertise needed to solve the problem when selecting team members. An effective leader cares about the team and the well-being of each team member. Caring about the team members creates positive and supportive conditions for working. Consider why someone would like to participate in your team and what would motivate them to contribute to the project's success.

What benefit would they get out of it? Also, think about how that person can justify that the project is a worthwhile cause and investment with an excellent return to the division or institution. Each member should get some benefit for contributing and being part of the team. This will lead to greater motivation to participate.

STRATEGIES FOR ASSEMBLING AN
INTERDISCIPLINARY TEAM TO SOLVE A PROBLEM

Visualize a Problem from a 360-Degree Perspective

- Identify the problem you are going to solve.
- Map out the problem you are going to address and examine the parts and pieces needed to solve the problem. Look at the problem from an interdisciplinary lens.
- Identify skills, expertise, and talents needed to solve the problem.
- Let your mind think about this issue over time, and refine your ideas.
- Be open to ideas when you travel to new places, meet new people. Let your thoughts germinate.
- Be mindful of new opportunities and interactions with people and resources that can lead to new possibilities.

Identify Potential Team Members

- When meeting people with interesting, diverse ideas and passion, be open to possibilities of collaboration.
- Engage in creative thinking by connecting ideas and individuals to create a spark for collaboration!

Select Team Members

- Choose team members that share passion and a common purpose.
- Read people; listen to your gut instinct to see if a potential team member is a good fit.
- Select team members who will work well together.
- Pick team members that you can trust.
- Select team members with a great attitude.
- Select team members with strong convictions so that they will go the distance.

Consider Why a Team Member Will Be Motivated to Participate

- Define people's roles within the team so that they know what is expected and how they can contribute.
- Support team members' aspirations.

NOTES

1. Mitchell Nathan and Karen Koellner, "A Framework for Understanding and Cultivating the Transition from Arithmetic to Algebraic Reasoning," *Mathematical Thinking and Learning* 9, no. 3 (2007): 179–92.

2. Principal investigator, "Understanding and Cultivating the Transition from Arithmetic to Algebraic Reasoning," sponsored by the Interagency Education Research Initiative (IERI; a collaboration of NSF, Dept. of Education—OERI/IES, and NIH-NICHHD; total award $5,798,281 Oct. 2001–Sept. 2006). (NSF 0115609, 0115635, and 0115661 under IERI collaborative research.) With co-PIs H. Borko, H. Kupermintz, J. Frykholm (University of Colorado), S. Derry, M. W. Alliable, and E. Knuth (University of Wisconsin–Madison), and K. R. Koedinger (Carnegie Mellon).

3. John Adiar, *The Art of Creative Thinking: How to Be Innovative and Develop Great Ideas* (London; Philadelphia: Kogan Page, 2009).

4. Howard Gardner, *Five Minds for the Future* (Boston: Harvard Business Review Press, 2009).

5. E. C. Wenger and W. M. Snyder, "Communities of Practice: The Organizational Frontier," *Harvard Business Review* 78, no. 1 (2000): 139–46.

6. Wenger and Snyder, "Communities of Practice."

7. Bill George, *Discover Your True North: Become an Authentic Leader*, 2nd ed. (Holbrook, NJ: John Wiley and Sons, 2015).

8. Daniel Goleman, Richard Boyatzis, and Annie McKee, *Primal Leadership: Unleashing the Power of Emotional Intelligence* (Boston: Harvard Business School, 2013).

9. Patrick Lencioni, *The Five Dysfunctions of a Team: A Leadership Fable* (San Francisco: Jossey-Bass, 2002).

10. James Kouzes and Barry Posner, *Leadership Challenge: How to Make Extraordinary Things Happen in Organizations*, 5th ed. (San Francisco: Jossey-Bass, 2012).

11. Dr. Kamil Jbeily, interview by Teruni Lamberg. All quotations of Dr. Jbeily in this book are from this interview.

THREE

How to Capitalize on Team Expertise

Teamwork is the ability to work toward a common vision.

—Andrew Carnegie

SHARE THE LEADER'S INITIAL VISION
WITH THE TEAM TO GET BUY-IN

Once a team is assembled, it is important to consider how the team can productively function together. The most important thing is that everyone understands the goal of the project and their individual role. The initial spark that brings a team together is the leader's vision. For example, Dr. Kamil A. Jbeily shared an excellent example of the role of the leader's vision. He pointed to an arbor that he had made to plant grapes in his backyard. He explained that as a child growing up in his homeland of Lebanon, he had fond memories of seeing bunches of grapes hanging from the vines in his parents' vineyard. He had built a six-foot wooden arbor to grow grapes. After building the arbor, he went to a nursery to buy the clippings to plant.

The worker in the nursery explained, "Dr. Jbeily, you are not going to get any fruits for about 4 to 5 years." Dr. Jbeily replied, "I know. I am aware of this." He visualized bunches and bunches of grapes hanging from his arbor. This motivated him to plant the garden despite the fact he would not get grapes until years later! He got home and communicated this vision to his wife and kids.

He inspired them to join him to tend the garden. This way they could enjoy the fruits as well. He reenacted the exercise of planting the clippings. He kneeled on the ground of his garden under the arbor and said, "As I was digging to plant the clippings, I was imagining/envisioning/visualizing/seeing/beholding the grapes hanging over me from the arbor, five years later!" He then smiled and said, "This is what I mean by vision!"

35

He emphasized that a leader should be able to visualize possibilities and communicate that vision to his team. He needed to communicate to his family his vision of grapes hanging from the arbor. In return, his family needed to understand the pleasure and the benefit they would get from growing, tending, and harvesting the fruit from their garden.

> Now, it is very important for the leader to see the grapes, to have a vision. . . . It is also important for my two daughters, my wife, and my son to see the grapes so that they can help me prune, fertilize, and cultivate the ground so that all of us will enjoy the grapes and achieve our shared vision. So, now, we are moving from the leaders' vision to the shared vision. This is a simple example of what vision is. . . .
>
> In growing your colleagues and partners in an organization, it is very important to enroll them into the vision and see what it takes to realize the vision. Most leaders can see the vision; they don't invest enough time to enroll their partners and colleagues into the vision.

Once the team gets together, the group should develop a shared vision. This is because your team members may have a different perspective of the common purpose. Furthermore, they may not know what other members are thinking either. Therefore, when you talk to each other, you can come up with a shared vision and understanding, so everyone is on the same page.

Dr. Barufaldi explained that you need a divergent team with different backgrounds and viewpoints. However, he stated that a common viewpoint is necessary for a group to function as a team:

> With a team, you can't always be divergent. You must come together with a common idea or goal. It is the divergence that is so interesting to me. I strongly encourage divergent thinking.

The leaders interviewed shared that their national and international accomplishments are attributed to team efforts. Synergistic teams can accomplish great things. Jon Katzenbach and Douglas Smith, who wrote *The Wisdom of Teams: Creating the High-Performance Organizations*, point out that a performance challenge brings a team together around a common goal.[1] This means that the team is working toward a common purpose to solve a problem. Everyone needs to have a shared understanding of vision and goals. First consider your vision, and then think about how to communicate the vision to the team.

CO-CREATE TEAM VISION

Ownership matters! When people feel ownership of the project, they are likely to put their heart and soul into the work. A vision brings everyone together. However, it is important that everyone is on the same page so that they can articulate and refine the vision. Dr. Paul Cobb pointed out an outstanding example of why the whole team needs to see the "big picture" and understand the significance of the work.[2]

He gave an example of a story from a book by Etienne Wenger titled *Communities of Practice, Learning, Meaning and Identity*.[3] He shared that many years ago, there were individuals cutting stones. When asked what they were doing, one person said that he was cutting stones. The other person said that he was building a cathedral. Dr. Cobb expressed that both individuals in the example were doing the same thing. However, the vision or understanding of *what* and *why* they were doing the cutting differed.

Would you rather be cutting stones for the sake of cutting stones, or would you rather be building a cathedral? This is like the story shared earlier by Dr. Jbeily. Both emphasized the importance of the leader communicating the vision and making sure the team understands the vision.

Katzenbach and Smith point out that the biggest ingredient of high-performing teams is *commitment*.[4] Team members need to feel ownership of the project and understand its significance. In other words, they need to see the "big picture." This way, each team member understands how his or her individual contribution supports the vision. In addition, they also understand the impact of the work on society.

Co-creating a shared vision based on the leader's vision allows each team member to provide input and shape the vision. It also provides opportunities for the team members to think about how the project aligns with their personal and professional goals. If a team member does not see value in the project, the chances are that the team member will simply lose interest or not put forth the effort.

Not every team member might have the same level of commitment. However, it is important to have a team where the majority is committed and passionate about the work. Face to face is the best way to create a team vision. When you are initially putting a team together, it might be necessary to do it through a phone conversation, some face-to-face interactions, and through e-mail if unable to meet as a group.

➤ *Communicate in person and through writing if unable to meet.*

A shared vision is necessary for a team to work toward a *common purpose*. In an ideal world, everyone is in the same room so that you can talk to each other. The reality may be that everyone is spread out in different physical and even geographic locations. This makes communication a challenge. Finding creative ways to communicate is needed when getting the project started. Think about how you can communicate the *common purpose* of the project with your team so that everyone has a shared understanding.

Case Study: The Nevada Mathematics Project

When writing the Nevada Mathematics Project grant proposal, I had to think about how to communicate with everyone. The Nevada Mathematics Project team was spread across the entire state of Nevada and several other states (six institutes of higher education, three Regional Training Centers, and every single school district in Nevada; this was a communication challenge). Geography, time, and even funding restricted the initial face-to-face communication.

Bringing the group together in the same room was not feasible. Therefore, I met with people individually, through phone conversations, and via e-mail. Even though I was meeting with individuals, the team members did not know each other.

The written document became an important artifact for communication. We shared the document back and forth and responded to comments in concrete ways. The document allowed us to verify each other's thinking and ask questions if something was unclear.

The Nevada Mathematics Project goals were influenced by the funders' grant proposal criteria. The funders' criteria became the focus of what we discussed. The written document became an important communication tool that everyone referred to when meeting face to face, individually, and in small groups and through phone conversations.

Even though everyone was not engaged in a two-way conversation, they got a sense of the "big picture" from the document, which captured the ongoing conversations. I became a mediator to clarify what we were each thinking. Sometimes discussions can remain vague and abstract if not documented in writing. Information was passed back and forth across organizational and geographic boundaries.

As the team leader, I understood the "big picture" and was communicating with individual team members or with small groups. At this point, we were functioning as a group of people trying to accomplish the task of writing the grant proposal. I would say that we were not quite functioning as a team yet. We had not all met yet as a team.

Team members did not know each other. In addition, they did not understand each other's expertise or perspective just yet. Becoming a team that functions synergistically together required a face-to-face meeting.

The planning meeting took place after the grant was funded. The planning meeting allowed us to meet as a team, understand each other's perspective, and lay out a plan to work together based on individual strengths. The planning meeting is where a team *identity* as the Nevada Mathematics Project team developed.

> ➤ *Develop shared understanding of vision through face-to-face communication.*

Face-to-face communication is ideal for developing a shared vision and a strategic plan. Getting together physically is especially important if the project gets funded, and you have work to do! This way everyone gets to know each other and understand each other's perspective. The face-to-face communication also provides opportunities for everyone to ask clarifying questions and give their input. In addition, it creates opportunities for developing personal relationships as well. Being on the same page is very helpful for functioning as a team. This is especially the case when work needs to be accomplished.

Case Study: The Nevada Mathematics Project

> Once our Nevada Mathematics Project was funded, we had enough funding to fly everyone down to Reno for a two-day intensive project meeting each year. The goal of the project meeting was to lay out the research agenda and plan high-quality STEM-integrated professional development for teachers. This face-to-face meeting was critical for everyone to know who was on the team. Because of geographic distance, people had not met each other, even though I knew each individual.

When a team comes together to solve a problem, a shared understanding of the problem situation is necessary. The common understanding allows them to communicate with each other through a shared language. In other words, it makes it possible to be on the same page because they understand each other's perspective. This is what Jeanne Lave and Etienne Wenger, who wrote a book on communities of practice, would call a "joint enterprise."

People work and function in different communities. Each community has different ways of thinking and functioning, which can sometimes create a commmuication challenge. For example, when individuals get together from different departments, organizations, grade levels, school districts, and so on, they might think and fuction differently.

For instance, if you are a teacher leader, you may find that your grade-level team thinks quite differently from another grade level. This makes it even more important that people meet and get together on the same page so that they understand each other's perpective.

Case Study: The Nevada Mathematics Project

> When the Nevada Mathematics Project team finally met, it was important to understand and recognize that each person belonged to different organizational communities such as colleges of education, colleges of science, school districts, Nevada Department of Education leaders, and Regional Training Centers across Nevada. Not everyone shared the same language or goals in our respective communities. Furthermore, people had different ways of communicating and functioning in their respective organizations.
>
> I knew that the stakes were high for this meeting. In two days, our goal was to lay out a plan for the summer institute that integrated everyone's

knowledge and was carefully sequenced to optimize teacher learning. Our goal was to support students to learn by helping teachers increase their content and pedagogical knowledge.

In addition to the goals of helping teachers, we also had the goal of laying out a research plan to study what we were doing. This was a lot to get accomplished in two days! I had to think about where we could even start. How do we ensure that everyone's voices are heard? I needed to think carefully about what we wanted to accomplish. We had pressing time constraints.

BECOME A LEARNING COMMUNITY

A team that learns together becomes a professional learning community. Learning together is an important part of generating new ideas and innovating. A leader sets the tone for communication and how people interact with each other. If people are uncomfortable sharing ideas and opinions, or if there is a power imbalance, then what gets created will not reflect the authentic thinking of the group.

Every team member, regardless of background, position, or credentials, should feel like a valued member of the team. Everyone has unique ideas, skills, and perspectives to contribute. The value of the team is the diversity of perspectives. This means that a leader must create conditions for positive interactions to occur. The goal is to make it possible for all team members to participate and contribute their ideas.

A nonthreatening environment is necessary for the creative process. People should not act in hierarchical roles; rather, they should feel free to express their thoughts and ideas honestly. The innovative leaders interviewed pointed out the importance of the team being able to share and communicate their ideas openly.

> ➢ *Have a dialogue, not a discussion.*

Communication is the key to creating the right conditions for freeflowing exchange of ideas. The focus of conversations should be on ideas, not egos.

Case Study: Nevada Mathematics Project

In the Nevada Mathematics Project meeting, it was important that each member felt appreciated. Furthermore, it was also important that everyone had equal power to share their ideas and have their voices heard. This process involved highlighting people's contributions and expertise, creating spaces for people's voices to be heard and used.

Valuing people's ideas requires having the right perspective, as stated by Dr. Jbeily:

> Everybody has something to offer, something you can utilize, develop, leverage, or synergize. Push the boundaries. Look for the good, praise it, and use it!

One of the things that Dr. Jbeily shared with me is how important communication is to any organization or team. He pointed out the difference between a *dialogue* and a *discussion*. He said that a dialogue is when people openly discuss things and share ideas. He noted that a "discussion is ego driven, driven by the self. A dialogue yields WIN-WIN results that are fueled by 'the we' and 'the us.'"

He said in a discussion that people are trapped by their position and opinion. They spend all their time justifying why their position or opinion is the right one. At the end of a discussion, rarely anything is accomplished. Discussions are driven by self-righteousness. In a dialogue, people suspend their positions and opinions and work together to come up with a better and improved way of doing things or running the organization, regardless of who gets the credit. Dialogues are driven by selflessness. According to Dr. Jbeily,

> I try to facilitate opportunities that advance dialogues rather than discussions. There is a huge difference between dialogues and discussions. In a dialogue, you, I, she, and he work together to come up with better ways of doing things in *our* oganization.

> ➢ *Have a plan, but be open-minded to ideas.*

Being open-minded and flexible is important for ideas to be shared and innovation to take place. An agenda is needed to keep things moving. However, it should be flexible and adaptable to achieve the tasks at hand. Dr. Richard Milner shared that a leader should have a plan in mind. However, it was important that the leader when working with the team also be open-minded. He also pointed out the importance of posing questions and validating people's ideas to make them comfortable to share. He, too, pointed out the importance of risk-taking for innovation:

> You need to have in your mind not *what* but *where* you want the discourse to lead. You have to pose questions and give people enough validation so that they can take a risk. Especially if you [as the leader in an organization] are the most senior person, people are looking at you to be the intellectual leader. Although they [newer team members] may have provocative ideas, some who are newer to the profession may be a bit timid; they may worry that the intellectual leader may not like something they said.

Dr. Milner pointed out that some people may lack the confidence to share their ideas or have a fear of expressing their opinion just in case others may not agree:

> What I do, I always try to validate the ideas even if a person is off target. I try to find some good in what folks are saying and verbalize it. This act of recognizing the strengths of comments makes people feel more comfortable sharing and risk-taking that the work goes to the next level of innovation. For some people, they have been told their entire life they are not quite adequate enough. Because of this, they may shut down when in fact they have much to offer.

Dr. Milner pointed out that hierarchical roles can be intimidating. Therefore, validating people's ideas and honoring people who are share ideas are important. A leader can only do this if he or she values the team member's contributions. In addition, each team member should feel valued by the entire team.

> ➤ *Validate people's ideas so that they feel safe to take risks.*

Think about what is needed to be accomplished and why. Keep the goals of the project as the center for making decisions. Dr. Milner's mission is to improve practices and the human condition. He pointed out that he kept true to his mission when running meetings. The focus of the group interaction is ultimately on what they are trying to achieve through the mission and vision of the work. According to Dr. Milner,

> We can critique all kinds of ideas, engage in interesting conversation, and challenge ideas. But at the end of the day, people have to remember the "why" of our work. They have to go back to the purpose behind the discourse. Leaders understand how to motivate team members to stay focused on what really matters most—practices, policies, and action that can impact and improve the human condition.
>
> This involves work in engaging in your own self-reflective moment, relaxing the ego, and trying to connect with other people. Realizing the work is not only about the students and teachers you are serving—it is also about members of the research team.
>
> It is important to realize that regardless of our state, or our educational level, we are all human beings trying to negotiate our emotions, challenges, struggles, and expectations.

Communication is key for developing a shared understanding. This requires thinking about the vision and re-creating it as a group through dialogue. Individual conversations may be great when getting started; however, to develop an identity and team spirit as a group, face-to-face communication is needed. Thinking about the human element of the team is helpful for creating a safe environment for communication. Having everyone on the same page to discuss ideas is important.

Case Study: Nevada Mathematics Project

In the Nevada Mathematics Project meeting, everyone shared their perspective about the goals of the project and how to achieve them. Once everyone had shared his or her perspective in the face-to-face meeting, we revisited the original vision and re-created it. We discussed what we wanted to keep and what we wanted to refine. The important part is that there was a conversation so that "common ground" was achieved. It also allowed us to understand and clarify each other's perspective.

The next section discusses the importance of listening to stakeholders. Before you come up with an action plan to carry out the vision, it is important to define the problem and ensure that it meets a need. Innovation is only useful if it meets the need of the people your team is going to serve.

Action Items

Strategies for developing a learning community:

➤ Have a dialogue, not a discussion.
➤ Have a plan, but be open-minded to ideas.
➤ Validate people's ideas so that they feel safe to take risks.
➤ A community of learners figures things out together.
➤ Re-create the vision as a group to ensure that everyone is on the same page and has a shared understanding.

STRATEGIES FOR IDENTIFYING A CHALLENGE AND CREATING A PLAN OF ACTION

➤ *Listen to stakeholders/customers that you serve to understand context and needs.*

Stakeholders/customers are very important. If you are designing an intervention to help someone, why don't you first figure out what their needs are and listen to their voices? Developing a solution without thinking about the problem is a waste of time. Stephen Covey, author of *The 8th Habit*, pointed out that seeing a problem is critical for making a difference.[5]

He talked about the power of paradigm. He gave an explanation as to why things don't change. People just don't see the problems in the first place. Identifying the problem and seeing what is happening is important. We must consider stakeholders' valuable insights, experiences, and knowledge.

Understanding the users'/customers' needs from their perspective is an important part of designing an intervention. A problem needs to be identified. You need to figure out *whom* you are serving. *What* is the context for the innovation? Has the real problem been identified? There is nothing worse than spending a whole lot of time coming up with a solution, only to discover that you did not come up with an adequate solution because the problem was not identified in the first place.

Prior to coming up with a solution, it is important to get to know the people you are serving and understand real needs from their perspective. For example, Dr. Megan Franke is a renowned mathematics education professor from UCLA who was recently elected to the National Academies. She shared the importance of listening to teachers and honoring their expertise and context they work in. She explained that when the team at the University of Wisconsin at Madison first started the Cognitively Guided Instruction project, they started out to develop tools and modules for teachers.

Dr. Franke was part of a research team at the University of Wisconsin at Madison that began to investigate how to share research on children's mathematical thinking (Cognitively Guided Instruction) with teachers. This work is widely used and has evolved over the past thirty years. We had introduced the Cognitively Guided Instruction thinking to our teachers in the first two years of the Nevada Mathematics Project. Dr. Jeff Shih, a professor at University of Nevada, Las Vegas, was instrumental in helping us implement this work. Dr. Shih had studied under Dr. Franke.

Dr. Franke explained that when the Cognitively Guided Instruction project was originally designed, it was to provide teachers with tools and units to implement in their classrooms. The team discovered through their research that teachers already knew a lot and had expertise that could be leveraged to support student learning. Their work was adapted over the years based on teachers' evolving needs and expertise.

The Cognitively Guided Instruction project thought about how to build on their joint expertise with their work with teachers. She pointed out the importance of tailoring the design and implementation of the intervention to the needs and concerns of the stakeholders/customers:

> In the initial experimental study, we had thought that we would give teachers examples of lessons and units that they could take and use. It was an initial proposal because it was too hard to tell teachers to figure this out all on

their own. The common notion at that time was to give them some materials they could use in their classroom.

When I started to develop some materials, it started to be really hard to do because it is not about the materials, right? So, having all the ideas of children's thinking built into the materials started to be really complicated. So, we decided at that point not to give them units but to help them create some units that they would use. You are the expert about this and you are going to see where it would go. You are the experts here![6]

Dr. Franke explained the importance of having the consumers drive innovation based on need:

You create this awesome learning opportunity where we had the opportunity to learn from really thoughtful smart teachers. So we did not really choose to do it the same way. So we got a chance to learn and they got a chance to drive things.

So I think after that first experimental study, because the teachers were driving it, teachers who were teaching second grade came to us and said: "Now, we don't know what to do. Because now we have children who are doing things way beyond. You have to help us now!"

So you have teachers who have been pushing the agenda to say. "Now you have to help us. It is your job! You can't leave it as a study and leave us. You have to help us figure out what to do." I don't think that would have happened if we had not made that initial shift in providing teachers that kind of power.

Dr. Barufaldi also pointed out the importance of having stakeholder input. He shared with me that he was working on a research proposal at the University of Texas at Austin that had to do with computer science. The team thought that they should work only with high-quality, high-level physics and math teachers. They said that there are a lot of people that are computer literate, but are not literate in science and technology. According to Dr. Barufaldi,

My suggestion was, Why don't you bring in teachers and other people from the community to build on this science project? It was to build a computer science professional development program within the community. So, I encouraged them to bring in a librarian who plays a crucial role, the PTA or the PTO to be part of the team, a parent, also qualified teachers and I also had them bring people from the "non-sciency" fields such as language arts and reading.

At this point, it was a very successful program in Texas. It was not just looking at these highly qualified skilled people that would become teachers of computer science. It was a team that came in from different perspectives, and I think that it contributed to the program becoming successful.

He had a difficult time selling the idea initially to the team. He pointed out the importance of getting input from the stakeholders in the community. The project became a success because of the critical feedback.

Case Study: Nevada Mathematics Project

This is why we started the Nevada Math Project planning meeting by having the district leaders, Nevada Department of Education leaders, and the regional trainers and teachers to provide details of the needs of the communities they serve. They shared what interventions worked and did not work. They identified specific things our institutes should address as connected to the grant proposal. (This sharing took place in the beginning of the planning meeting.)

Not only that, but they were instrumental in giving feedback and shaping the institutes. We made sure that we listened to them and learned about what they were doing and noticing and observing. During this time, everyone listened and asked questions for clarification. Each member at the meeting had prepared a PowerPoint slide or handout so that people had hard copies of what they were talking about. The next section describes what we accomplished in the planning meeting. Based on input from the stakeholders, we developed a strategic action plan.

➤ *Develop a strategic action plan.*

Once a vision is co-created, then tasks must be identified and assigned. Katzenbach and Smith point out that a team needs a clear understanding of performance outcomes and results to function and accomplish things as a team. Katzenbach and Smith also write that a team approach involves integrating talents and skills.[7] Consider what needs to be accomplished in a planning meeting when the team gets together. There is nothing more frustrating than being part of a team and not knowing what you are supposed to be doing!

The following example from the Nevada Mathematics Project illustrates the process used in the planning meeting to set the vision and to come up with a plan of action. This case study is intended as a tool to think about how you might accomplish your tasks. This does not mean that the format presented below needs to be followed. Rather, a planning meeting must be structured around the project goals. Project goals and team members' contributions should be clearly articulated.

Case Study: Nevada Mathematics Project

The goals and outcomes of the meeting were made explicit ahead of time so that everyone knew what we needed to accomplish by the end of the second day. The planning meeting was structured to make sure voices were heard.

Specifically, people shared their thoughts and expertise and the group listed and asked questions.

There were opportunities for people to get into groups and brainstorm ideas around the problems posed. The brainstorming sessions allowed multiple perspectives and knowledge to come together to solve a problem and come up with a product. The goal of this meeting was to figure out a way to come up with a plan for the institutes where everyone's knowledge and skill was integrated.

The agenda for the meeting is listed in table 3.1. Notice that the outcomes of the meeting are clearly stated. Opportunities were structured for people to share information, get to know each other formally and informally, and have work time to collaborate and come up with ideas. The meeting ended with a summary of action items.

Table 3.1. Project Meeting Agenda

Nevada Mathematics Project Meeting Agenda

Project Meeting Goals

Design high-quality summer institutes and follow-up sessions to optimize teacher learning of the Nevada Academic Content Standards based on the Common Core and the Next Generation Science Standards: Science & Technology, Physical Science and Personal and Social Perspectives (NGSS). Take into account how to support shifts in teacher practice to support student learning. The mathematics content focus will be measurement and data analysis for grades K–5 and geometry and data analysis for grades 6–8. This content will be embedded in the NGSS with a special focus on nanotechnology. (See unit at the end of document.)

- Understand the needs of Nevada teachers and students so that the design of PD is responsive to regional needs.
- Capitalize expertise of the team.
- Carefully sequence activities and tasks so that they meaningfully build on each other.
- Develop an agenda so that each team member is clear about their role and what they will be doing. Have a shared understanding of what the team will be doing.
- Identify any materials or handouts that need to be printed.
- Clarify research goals to study what we are doing to inform current and future projects. Specifically, IRB approval.
- Develop a three-ring binder for project team members to use so that we know what we are all doing. Goal: Become a learning community.

Schedule

May 31

- 8:30–9:00: Coffee and breakfast—team members get to informally chat with each other.
- 9:00–9:15: Introductions
- 9:15–9:30: Goals of project
- 9:30–10:30: Identify local, regional needs and needs of Nevada students, and get an understanding of what works/doesn't work for students and teachers.

(continued)

Table 3.1. *Continued*

- ○ Dave Brancamp: Nevada Department of Education goals/student performance across grades—understand current student performance of students in math and science across K–8 grade levels.
- ○ Denise Trakas, Vicki Collaro, and Lucy Gillette: Share needs of the district, what works, what does not work. Identify needs of district and things that work within local regional sites. (A bulleted handout would be great.)
- ○ Tina Westwood, Kathy Dees, and Kathy Lawrence: Thoughts about how to encourage teachers to put into practice what they have learned in the institutes. Insights or needs of what works or does not work. (A bulleted list would be nice if this can be shared.)

- 10:30–10:50: Break, take group photo. UNR Communications is doing a story of our project.
- 10:40–11:00: Refine and develop clear goals/outcomes of the professional development content knowledge we want to ensure teachers get from the institutes—relate to CCSS and NGSS standards. What pedagogical knowledge do we want teachers to develop—specific focus?
- 11:00–11:30: Goal: Develop a schedule to structure the summer institutes. (See attached document—revise as group.) Sequencing of math and science content/pedagogical content/collaboration time
- 12:00–1:00: Lunch

- ○ Goal: Higher education team and business partner share research and tasks that will be conducted in the PD sessions. This way, the team has an idea of each sequence, and the PD has a clear flow.

- 1:00–2:00: Robert Chang and Mathew Hsu—share ideas and do a sample activity to illustrate Nano Modules. Share what type of evaluation can be used to measure teacher learning.
- 2:00–2:15: Break
- 2:15–3:00: Mitchell Nathan—share research on gestures and share a task with the group that will be conducted as part of the institute. Also plans for research.
- 2:30–2:45: Break
- 2:45–3:30: Travis Olson, Ed Keppelman, Teruni Lamberg, and Steven Demelin—share some tasks and ideas to be conducted in the summer institutes (handouts helpful).
- 3:30–3:40: Craig Wall—share thoughts about how to integrate the business/industry perspective into the PD design. How can we think about how to prepare students to think about careers of the future? What are some current technologies, and how can they prepare students for the future?
- 3:45-4:00: Wrap-up—identify what worked and what we need to work on tomorrow.

June 1

- 8:00–8:30: Informal coffee (networking time)
- 8:30–9:00: Revisit sequencing if we need to adjust the activities (Tina and Lucy and others share any ideas of tasks to be conducted in PD session.)

- 9:00–10:00: Collaboration time—break out into math, science, and district and RPDP groups. (Identify and narrow down specific tasks that will be conducted in the PD sessions.)
  - ○ Math: Narrow down tasks and ensure that the project-based learning idea of nanotechnology is used as a context when possible.
  - ○ Science: Narrow down tasks to be used in institutes
  - ○ District leaders and RPDP: Decide how to capitalize on district/RPDP goals to support teachers to improve their instruction. District leaders and RPDP have more in-depth knowledge and relationships at the local level. What kinds of supports can be put in place? Feedback on the effectiveness of PD.
- 10:00–10:15: Break
- 10:15–12:00: Whole-group discussion, revisit timeline, and narrow down tasks.
- 12:00–1:45: Lunch? (Could finish early.)
- 1:45–2:00: Goals for follow-up session; identify topics that will adapt and build from summer institutes. Evaluation? Student content tests, teacher tests, etc. Clarify research plan for Project.

Question to think about: Do we start with data analysis/statistics and then do geometry? Do we integrate both? The Nano Modules have carefully aligned NGSS and the math.

Credit: Teruni Lamberg.

Think About . . .

Running a Planning/Project Meeting

- ➤ What are you trying to accomplish?
- ➤ Are the goals clear to the group?
- ➤ What is the group vision?
- ➤ How are you going to structure your meeting so everyone's voice is heard?
- ➤ What do you expect everyone to prepare ahead of time?
- ➤ How are you going to ensure group feedback is given?
- ➤ Do you need break-out time for people to solve problems in smaller groups?
- ➤ Do you have unstructured meeting time for informal conversations?
- ➤ What tools and materials do you need (space, technology, etc.)?
- ➤ Who is going to take notes/record the meeting?
- ➤ What products do you want at the end of the meeting?
- ➤ End the meeting by figuring out "actions items" to be accomplished.
- ➤ Document group thinking.

> ➤ *Break into smaller groups to tackle tasks, but connect to the big picture.*

When planning/facilitating breakout groups or working on smaller tasks, it is important that the smaller teams check in to ensure their work fits with the larger goal and what everyone else is doing. I remember this point being hit hard when I was in high school. In high school, I was part of a Junior Achievement program sponsored by IBM where we got to run our own company. They trained us how to run a business.

In one of the training sessions, our mentors asked us to design a toy doll. They split us into groups and assigned us different tasks. Each small group had to come up with a design for parts of the doll. One group worked on the head, the other the legs, and so on. We were so engaged in what we were doing. The teams were even competing to develop the best part. Some did not want others to see what they were doing.

We all worked hard in our group as our IBM sponsors walked around smiling. After our time was up, they asked us to share what we did. They cut out our model drawings and assembled the doll. There were squeals of laughter when we realized that the individual parts might have been brilliant, but when the doll was assembled, it looked more like a Frankenstein doll. The doll body was out of proportion. The parts did not fit.

> ➤ *Align small-group tasks with the "big picture."*

A valuable lesson that day was that we needed to communicate with the other teams to deliver a product that was useful. There was no restriction placed on us to talk with others. However, no one got up to ask questions. We all jumped into our task right away. I am grateful that I am in touch with Charlie Arroyo, who was one of my mentors from IBM. He provided valuable feedback on this manuscript. I am thankful to IBM and the Junior Achievement program to have been mentored as a high school student to think about leadership.

ADAPT PROJECT TO EXPERTISE AND EXPERTISE TO PROJECT

Do what you love and love what you do!

—Teresa Amble

When we can carve out a piece of work and take the initiative, we feel a sense of ownership. Dr. Paul Cobb pointed out that it is a two-way relationship. People should have an interest and identify with the work and have expertise in the area. He also noted that the work must also benefit the project outcomes and goals. Most importantly, the team member must adapt to the project, and the project must adjust to the team members' interests and expertise. He gave an example of hiring a postdoc to work on his team:

> We tried to be brutally honest about the nature of the data that we were collecting, and we wanted her to provide the leadership and equity aspect and support her too as opportunity arose with a small NSF grant.
> But it would mean for her not to do straight ethnography but collaborating with people on other things and methodology, which she was up for. So, it worked out well. So, *she* had to adapt, and *we* had to adapt, if you follow me. . . . As people come along, you adapt the project. It goes with particular directions that fit with their interests.

Think about your role as a team member. What team have you been part of recently? You may find that you want to know clearly what your role in the project team is and the tasks you are expected to complete. If you are unclear what your role is, then it can demotivate you to participate because you are unclear about how you should be contributing.

> ➤ *Match expertise to task, and adapt project to expertise.*

Similarly, as Dr. Paul Cobb pointed out, the project should build on the team members' strengths, and the team member should adapt to the project. Matching tasks with expertise is important. For example, in the Nevada Mathematics Project, Dr. Chang, Dr. Hsu, and Dr. Wall were experts in nanotechnology. Therefore it made sense for them to take the lead in teaching and to organize the nanotechnology tasks in the Nevada Mathematics Project.

The math educators had expertise in how children learn math and teach math. So, it makes sense for these team members to think about how to integrate the math into the professional development. When you capitalize on team members' expertise, then you get a better outcome.

Dr. Teresa Amabile from Harvard, who is known for her work in creativity, wrote: "Maintaining your creativity in your work depends on maintaining your intrinsic motivation. This means two things. You should do what you love, and you should love what you do. The first is a matter of doing the work that matches well with your expertise, your creative thinking skills, and your strongest intrinsic motivation."[8]

Each person should have a clearly defined role that can be adaptive to the situation. The clearly defined roles make it easier and more efficient to work because each person understands what their contribution to the project is and pragmatically what they need to be doing. Clearly defined roles avoid frustration and wasted time.

One of the biggest challenges in running any project is managing time and efficiency. When team members know what is expected and can articulate their role, they will be able to function more efficiently. This is particularly the case if team members have competing demands on their time.

> ➤ *Get to know each team member personally.*

Getting to know each team member personally helps. One way is to have informal conversations with potential team members and understand what their personal and professional contexts are for participating in the project. Understanding individual perspectives will give you a sense of their realistic time commitment and professional goals for taking part in the project. Understand how each person is recognized in their institution or department.

The goal is to build on the team member's expertise and strengths and to support professional goals as well. You can thoughtfully ensure that each team member benefits from participating in the project. Think about possible rewards and recognition to help team members feel valued as part of your team and also the context in which they work.

Dr. Ana de Bettencourt-Dias, a scientist in the Nevada Mathematics Project, wanted to participate so that she could build a capacity or mechanism for outreach. She was thinking about how this project could help her get funding for other research she was conducting as well.

This is a different context than a school district coordinator whose job is to provide professional development to teachers. When having these members as part of my team, it was important to ensure that each person's needs were valued and met within the project. Therefore, there is a reason why someone would want to participate.

Your goal is to make sure that each team member's time and expertise are valued and considered. Each team member needs to see the benefits of the project personally as well as the larger goal. This information is valuable when conceptualizing each team member's role and contribution in the project and jointly creating and defining a vision.

Think About . . .

➤ Ask your team member about their expertise and how they would like to contribute to the project.
➤ Adapt the project so that it aligns with people's expertise. (Recruit people who have expertise appropriate for the project.)
➤ Ensure that team members understand the "big picture" so that they can adapt to the project.

Defining each member's role within the team is essential for clarity of roles also; each team member needs to know what specific tasks need to be accomplished. Furthermore, supporting personal goals is something that needs to be considered for team members to be committed to the work.

CHAPTER SUMMARY

Create a blueprint for success!
The team can function because they know their larger purpose and individual contributions!

Once you have assembled a team, a plan is needed to carry out the work. This means you initially brought a team together based on your vision. Once you have the team together, they need to own the vision and believe in it. They need to be excited about the possibilities. This means the vision must be revisited and co-created with the team considering the expertise of the team and the goals of the project.

You need to build excitement to participate in the project so that you have committed team members. This means motivating your team members by having them take ownership for part of the work. You need to ensure that the tasks that are assigned are matched with expertise and interests. Everyone needs to see the value of their contribution and how it fits into the "big picture."

Dialogue is a critical part of building a learning community. An effective team must function as a learning community so that the team learns from each other and capitalizes on the expertise of the team. Create conditions for people to take risks, share their ideas, and build on each other's expertise. You are the team leader; the experts in your team play different instruments. How you structure the interactions will determine if you create a beautiful symphony or if there is disharmony.

Recognize, appreciate, and value your team members. The project must adapt to the individual, and the individual must adapt to the project. Consider each person's personal and professional goals and support their aspirations in the project. This will motivate the person to participate because they are part of something greater.

The leader should create mechanisms for communication so that everyone's contribution is valued so that the environment is nonthreatening. A project that has excellent communication and builds on team members' strength through communication and tasks optimizes conditions for success.

STRATEGIES FOR CAPITALIZING
ON TEAM EXPERTISE TO GET BUY-IN

Develop a Vision

- A leader initially shared his or her vision to get buy-in.
  - ◦ Communicate in person and through writing the initial vision if unable to meet.
- Have a plan, but be open to ideas.

Co-Create Vision and Mission with Team

- Once the team is assembled, the vision must be re-created so that the team has a shared sense of purpose and ownership of the project.
  - ◦ Develop a shared understanding of the vision through face-to-face communication.
  - ◦ Become a learning community.
  - ◦ Have a dialogue, not a discussion—this means everyone must share ideas and listen to each other.
  - ◦ Validate people's ideas so that they feel safe to take risks.

Identifying a Challenge

- Listen to stakeholders/customers that you serve to understand context and needs.

Run a Planning Meeting

- Develop a strategic action plan—figure out what needs to be done and when, and assign tasks.
- Consider the following when organizing and conducting a project planning meeting:
  - ◦ Ensure the team understands the "big picture" and their role within it.
  - ◦ What are you trying to accomplish?
  - ◦ Does the group understand the goals of the meeting?
  - ◦ What is the group vision?
  - ◦ How are you going to structure your meeting so everyone's voice is heard?
  - ◦ What do you expect everyone to prepare ahead of time?
  - ◦ How are you going to ensure group feedback is given?
  - ◦ Do you need break-out time for people to solve problems in smaller groups?

- ○ Do you have unstructured meeting time for informal conversations?
- ○ What tools and materials do you need? (Space, technology, etc.)
- ○ Who is going to take notes / record the meeting?
- ○ What products do you want at the end of the meeting?

Adapt the Project to Expertise, and Adapt Expertise to the Project

- Get to know each team member personally.
- Plan to communicate with everyone.
- Build a nonthreatening environment of communication and building of ideas.
- Support personal and professional aspirations of team members.

NOTES

1. Jon Katzenbach and Douglas Smith, *The Wisdom of Teams: Creating the High-Performance Organizations* (Boston: Harvard Business Review Press, 1993).

2. Dr. Paul Cobb, interview by Teruni Lamberg. All quotations of Dr. Cobb in this book are from this interview.

3. Etienne Wenger, *Communities of Practice: Learning, Meaning, and Identity* (Cambridge: Cambridge University Press, 1998).

4. Katzenbach and Smith, *The Wisdom of Teams*.

5. Stephen R. Covey, *The 8th Habit: From Effectiveness to Greatness* (London: Simon and Schuster, 2014).

6. Dr. Megan Franke, interview by Teruni Lamberg. All quotations of Dr. Franke in this book are from this interview.

7. Katzenbach and Smith, *The Wisdom of Teams*.

8. Teresa Amabile, "Motivating Creativity in Organizations: On Doing What You Love and Loving What You Do," *California Management Review* 40, no. 1 (1997): 55.

FOUR

How to Create Conditions to Generate Innovative Ideas

I roamed the countryside searching for the answers to things I did not understand. Why shells existed on the tops of mountains along with the imprints of coral and plant and seaweed usually found in the sea. Why the thunder lasts a longer time than that which causes it and why immediately on its creation the lightening becomes visible to the eye while thunder requires time to travel. How the various circles of water form around the spot which has been struck by a stone and why a bird sustains itself in the air. These questions and other strange phenomena engaged my thought throughout my life.

—Leonardo da Vinci

A leader needs to create conditions to optimize the flow of creative ideas. What do you love to do? Perhaps you love to paint, or read, plant a garden, or play chess? Think about something that truly excites you. Have you ever found yourself so immersed in doing something that you find terribly interesting and discover that you had lost all sense of time? Was there skill involved in that task? Why were you so motivated to work on it despite its difficulty and challenges?

The experience that you just thought about is what Dr. Mihaly Csikszentmihalyi—an expert on creativity—calls a *flow* experience. He wrote a book titled *Creativity and Flow and the Psychology of Discovery and Invention*.[1] He described this state as an enjoyable experience where people are so immersed in what they are doing that they persist despite challenges. A key component of *flow* is that the right challenge and skills are matched along with the person's interest. When people experience a state of *flow*, they persist despite the challenges.

Think about how you can create conditions so that your team engages with the project. How can you facilitate the creative flow of ideas so that your team can generate ideas and innovate? Charles Palus and David Horth wrote an article in the *Ivey Business Journal* titled "Leading Creatively: The Art of Making Sense."[2] In this article, they point out that creative leadership is an art form that is part analytical and part artistry.

According to them, these conditions are needed to create new and innovative ideas and products.

HAVE A POSITIVE AND SUPPORTIVE ATTITUDE

➤ *The team leader cares about the team members as individuals.*

The leaders' attitude and how they treat people matter. Would you rather work in a team where the leader cares about you and is supporting your success as well as the team's success? Or would you prefer to work with someone who does not care about you? The leader's attitude influences the team productivity and the dynamics of the environment to be creative and take risks.

Dr. Jbeily pointed out that the leader must *value* and *appreciate* people. He shared that when you take the time to listen, take the time to care about people as individuals, it creates conditions for performance. He also mentioned that you need to create opportunities for your team members to shine, and he even went as far as stating that you need to care for your team members' security. In other words, he meant psychological, emotional, and career goals, among others:

> The best investment you make in people is their capacity. Everyone has something good to offer. Everyone wants to do the best that they can do. Everyone has something good to offer; the key is how you can invest in it and capitalize on it. Make people believe in themselves, recognize them, honor them, appreciate them, give them security, and give them the challenge of dealing with everyday life in a way that is stimulating and exciting.

> It is all about *investing in other people.* You get what you invest in people! You get what you put in a pot when you cook. If you put good stuff, quality material, you are going to get a meal. If you give the love, the attention, and the enjoyment, you are going to get a good meal. *It is always about investment and return.*

Great leaders throughout history are ones who serve others such as Martin Luther King, Gandhi, and so on. Dr. Howard Gardner and Dr. Emma Laskin in their book *Leading Minds* point out that leaders throughout history who have made a profound difference can influence people with their stories. They can influence people because they live consistent lives that "embody" their stories. Gardner and Laskin explain that the leaders who were historically successful had *followers* who were receptive to the story.[3]

What are your thoughts about leadership? Which type of leader are you? Think about a leader whose qualities motivated you to do your best.

Now reflect on a leader who has demotivated you. What are some of the characteristics of these leaders?

What qualities do you think were helpful? The bottom line is the leader's attitude influences the dynamics of the team. What type of leadership style allows you to be most creative and productive? A leader needs to create a safe environment where people feel valued so that they can take risks and contribute in novel ways.

Advice from Dr. Kamil A. Jbeily

1. *Appreciate* and *value* people.
2. Create opportunities for people to shine and a stimulating environment.
3. Offer people security for their family, their career, and so on.
4. Have a win-win attitude!

Dr. Jbeily had wonderful insight about interacting with others. He talked about having an *abundant mentality*. What he meant by this is that people must become *selfless*. They must value others and treat people well.

> If you as a partner, colleague, or organization recognize that there is an interest in investing in you and believing in you, and giving you every opportunity to excel, everybody wants to work with you.
>
> That is a problem in many organizations, that selfless work and the ability to invest in other people, and become and think pragmatically, and saying, "If I am working with Teruni and Teruni is in good shape, I am in good shape." We are partners; we are engaging in a win-win relationship. That is the premise of what I call an *abundance mentality* as opposed to a *scarcity mentality*.

➤ *The leader thinks positively and has an abundance mentality.*

One of the themes that emerged from a conversation with Dr. Jbeily was the importance of positive thinking. My father was a great advocate of positive thinking, dreaming and visualizing the impossible. This was something he emphasized growing up, the importance of positive thinking. I wondered what that had to do with leadership. I realized that being able to have a sense of gratitude and wake up every day feeling thankful is a healthy way to live. When you are happy as a leader and are joyful, it is easier to care about others. Dr. Jbeily also echoed this same feeling:

> Look at nature. Look at the mountains in Reno and see how vast, how ubiquitous they are; how can you see with the scarcity mentality when you see the abundance of nature? That is why I encourage my kids to open the blinds

and see outside; look at nature and see how beautiful it is! How can you not have the abundance mentality?

The *abundance mentality* is the healthiest and the most important thing that people can cultivate in themselves, and most importantly help others cultivate that in themselves.

Dr. Jbeily's beliefs are reflected in the five values of the Texas Regional Collaborative he founded. He shared that this program ran with five simple values. He constantly asked himself if he and his team were being faithful to their values. These values included the following:

1. *Serve* the customers such as teachers.
2. *Treasure* your people—people who work for you, your secretary, the professor, you should treasure, and give them the opportunities and value them.
3. *Operate with integrity*—for example, provide courses to teachers to serve a need, not to make money.
4. *Reward your partners*—you must show that people are invested in you, and they are getting an excellent return on their investment.
5. *Contribute to systematic reform*—transform education!

Louis Baron wrote an article on authentic leadership and mindfulness development through action learning.[4] In this article, he writes that the authentic leader is self-aware about her strengths and weaknesses as they relate to values, beliefs, and emotions and how they affect others. The authentic leader can share genuine emotions and look at information in an unbiased manner along with an internalized moral perspective.

He also points out that authentic leadership can be developed through mindfulness training and reflection. Mindfulness involves being present and paying attention to the moment and becoming self-aware. Adam Perlman—who wrote an article on "Informed Mindfulness as the Foundation for Leadership"—writes that when you are self-aware and reflect, it leads to a more informed state.[5] This informed state leads to making better decisions. This way, a leader is not acting out of emotions or reacting to situations. The leader can think about her core values and the vision of the project and make decisions that make sense and move the project forward.

> ➢ *Being authentic and mindful involves having a relatively low ego.*

An interesting finding of being mindful and being authentic involves having a relatively low ego. Whitney L. Heppner and Michael H. Kernis wrote an article on "'Quiet Ego' Functioning" in which they write that research has proven this link.[6] The ego was a topic that emerged several times in interviews with several influential leaders. It was much easier to work with people who are not driven by egos.

The leaders that were interviewed in this book felt that it was important to be authentic. They genuinely cared about making a difference and supporting others. They focused less on the ego and more about making a difference or discovering something they were curious about.

DEVELOP EXPERTISE BY DEVELOPING KNOWLEDGE WITHIN THE FIELD, RELATED FIELDS, AND REAL-WORLD EXPERIENCES

> I have a special talent. I am passionately curious.

> —Albert Einstein

> ➤ *Innovative leaders are lifelong learners.*

Continuous improvement and growth are necessary to become a great leader. Improving is to challenge yourself to develop the skills and attributes for leadership. Dr. Jbeily pointed out how important it is to "develop true nobility":

> If we look at others and compare ourselves, it is not a healthy way. It is important to aspire to be the best, aspire your perspective from comparing yourself to yourself. Thinking about yourself. Thinking that yourself tomorrow is going to be better than yourself today.
>
> Conformity is the ultimate "dwarfer." It is important to cultivate in our children and ourselves what I call "true nobility," which is not trying to be better than someone else. *It is being better today than what you were yesterday.*

> ➤ *Innovative leaders develop expertise.*

Leaders must strive to develop expert knowledge to lead. Expert knowledge allows the leader to notice things, make decisions, and connect information in novel ways. The process of developing expertise involves a combination of experience and intensive reading and study of things. Experts and novices notice things differently.

The leader's decisions are influenced by his or her knowledge and experiences. A leader can make connections and solve problems differently. A study on expert and novice chess players is described in the book by the National Research Council titled *How People Learn: Brain, Mind, Experience and School.*[7] The expert chess player can look at the board and see multiple patterns, whereas the novice might focus on a couple of pieces in front of him. The authors of the book write that experts can notice patterns and information not noticed by novices. Also, they have a lot more knowledge that allows them to see patterns and make connections.

The role of expertise was something worth exploring with the innovative leaders interviewed. How did their knowledge and expertise compare with the expert chess players? These innovative leaders had developed expertise and were able to see intricate patterns. Expertise was developed through experience, reading, and study of a field along with various other fields that they found intriguing over their careers.

In other words, they had an interdisciplinary view of things. Dr. Cobb was aware of the chess study. He mentioned that "chess players look ahead, but they look at patterns and so on." The next section describes ways innovative leaders develop expertise.

> ➢ *Innovative leaders learn through experience. This experience allows them to have a point of reference to make sense of things.*

Learning through *experience* is powerful because it provides practical knowledge that cannot be attained through reading alone. You may read about something, but it is much more powerful if you have experiences to connect it to. The innovative leaders interviewed were not just ivory tower academics, but they were in the trenches learning about things through experience. They traveled along with their research teams and were out in the field learning from experience.

Experience combined with book knowledge or theory results in powerful learning. Most of the leaders that were interviewed in this book work in education. These individuals work with teachers, visit classroom settings, and are engaged in "hands-on" research along with their research teams. They could very easily relegate this fieldwork to graduate students since it is time-consuming. However, they strongly feel that this type of experience is valuable for them and the team.

That is why Dr. Paul Cobb traveled with the team as we conducted professional development and research. He was an extremely busy man, but he took the time to do this! Dr. Cobb mentioned that it was important to have real-world contexts such as classrooms, districts, and schools to work with and think with as he read stuff. He had a frame of reference to draw from:

> This is why I do it, so that it is not abstract, disembodied texts. Things that resonate for me are things I read that allow me to look at something that I am familiar with or think I know in a very different way.

Dr. Megan Franke also talked a lot about her interactions with teachers. She visited many schools and worked with them. She had teachers try out a research-based innovation that her team had created and took the time to learn how the innovation was used. Listening and working with teachers in the field was vital to her learning.

There is a beautiful children's story written by Leo Lionni titled *Fish Is Fish*.[8] The story is about a friendship between a fish and tadpole. The tadpole disappears because he has turned into a frog. The frog leaves the pond, explores the world, and tells the fish about the flying birds he has seen and other things. The fish envisions a bird as a fish with wings.

The interesting point about this story is that you need experience as a frame of reference to make sense of things. Think about the kinds of experiences you have had, and how they help you figure things out. What kind of experiences do you need to successfully innovate in your project?

> *Experience combined with knowledge is important for professionally noticing.*

Experience combined with noticing things and reflection leads to powerful learning experiences. Otherwise, you may not even notice things that you experience. As Dr. Paul Cobb mentioned, it is important to connect what you read and study to experience. At the same time, you must be open to seeing things in a new way.

For example, you may be looking at a classroom and not noticing things even though you are physically there. Victoria Jacobs, Lisa Lamb, and Randolph Philipp wrote an article on how teachers *professionally notice* children's mathematical thinking. They point out that noticing is both complex and challenging.[9]

Therefore, paying attention to things and thinking about what you are noticing and not noticing is important. Furthermore, you must make a connection between your experiences and what you are thinking about. Dr. Rochelle Gutiérrez provided her perspective of how her lived experiences influenced her research. She drew from her experience to make a difference:

I think what is true of all research is that we bring our lived experiences to the research process: as a woman, as a mother, and all these things that I am. When I am listening to things my participants are saying in interviews or when I am observing a classroom or whenever I am doing any form of research, I already have my lenses that I have formulated that are familiar to me. So, when I go into that space, I will see something that other people may not see, and others may see things that I may not see.

There is no neutral process; this is entirely subjective and related to who the researcher is. The first part of doing great research is recognizing and embracing that. We are always positioned in our research, even if we do not make it explicit.

Creative insubordination was something that I was familiar with at a personal level. It was not a research thing; it was not something that I had read;

it was not something I learned from a grad school article. It was something that I knew on a personal level. Having been raised in an activist family, I was taught that when you are trying to uphold the values of dignity for another person or you are trying to address a social injustice, you sometimes have to ask someone in power to go along with what you want to do, and not just follow the rules.

And, if you asked someone to do something because it was the right thing, because it addressed social justice, and they said no, you did not just accept that. Instead, you would nod politely, and then you would move around that person and find some other person that you could talk to who could help you accomplish what you wanted. You were creatively insubordinate.

The whole notion of bending the rules or the procedures was being modeled all the time. It was modeled in a way by my parents and the people around me. They were always holding themselves to this higher ethical standard. It is not what you are supposed to do because it was school policy or this is not what the neighborhood group has decided is important. It is like, *how do you look at yourself in the mirror every day and say, "I am happy," and be proud of who I am and what I stand for at the end of the day?*

So, when I prepare teachers for the work of teaching, that is what I am doing. I am writing a book called the *Mirror Test* that explores the politics of teaching mathematics and how we might redefine what it means to be a "professional" not externally by students' standardized test scores or outside teacher evaluations developed by corporations, but internally with a sense of the ethical compass and wanting to advocate for students even when it means taking risks in the classroom, school, or district.

I am asking teachers to say, "Can I look in the mirror and reflect on what I am doing every day and ask myself 'Is this what I said I would do when I entered this profession? And, if it's not, what am I going to do about that?'" Maybe this mirror test is related to my life; I went from biology to education. I feel a great sense of responsibility for learners and teachers because everything I do can make a difference. So, if I don't do it with my heart, and I don't do well, I can't look myself in the mirror. I'm always asking myself, "Am I being consistent with what I believe?" If I am not, then it is just as bad as messing up a surgery. Because it will have a lasting effect on the rest of their lives and that can't just be fixed by another procedure.

What field are you in? What experiences have you had to make sense of stuff you are working on? What are your lived experiences and how do you draw from them in your work? What kind of experiences do you need to enhance your learning? Think about what you are seeing and experiencing. Pay attention! Connect it to other experiences and things you have been reading about. Especially consider what kind of experiences you need in your project to solve problems.

> ➤ *Innovative leaders read a lot and study stuff before they embark on a new project.*

"The old saying that knowledge is power still holds true," said Dr. Paul Cobb. He emphasized that practical, experiential knowledge and reading and studying the field are important, as illustrated in figure 4.1. He also reads a lot of stuff from graduate students, writings from other scholars, along with many kinds of readings. I would categorize his readings as follows: disciplinary readings, interdisciplinary readings, and thoughts. Disciplinary readings had to do with his field; interdisciplinary readings had to do with fields that he finds relevant and interesting.

The other kind of readings were responding to people's ideas and reading stuff that might have been half-baked ideas. I had to admit that I sent him a lot of half-baked ideas to read when I was his postdoc, and he quickly responded to my thinking and challenged me to think deeper. As I reflected on it, this was a wonderful feedback loop between him and me. So, the ideas were continually brainstormed, reflected, and revised.

Dr. Megan Franke shared that sometimes she assigns readings to her graduate students and they read them and send her e-mails even before they had time to meet. As I reflected on this, I realized how important it is to consider reading people's thoughts and ideas about things, even if it is scratched on a sheet of paper or through e-mails. If you only read well-developed thoughts, it does not leave a space to think about the novel or

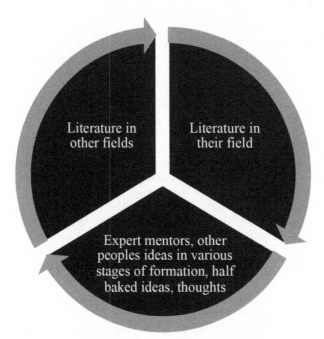

Literature in other fields

Literature in their field

Expert mentors, other peoples ideas in various stages of formation, half baked ideas, thoughts

Figure 4.1.   Innovative Leaders' Knowledge and Experiences
Credit: Teruni Lamberg.

new ideas even if they are half-baked. It also gives you opportunities to challenge ideas presented and ask questions to take it to the next level.

Innovative leaders are not limited by tunnel vision such as only one discipline. They can view the landscape or, as we say, the forest while trying to focus on a tree. They think about things from multiple perspectives and even disciplines. This required an interdisciplinary lens. I asked Dr. Cobb to give an example of what he read and how that influenced his work. He gave an example of how the field of literacy influenced his dissertation study on how children learned math:

> I read what I find interesting. I am giving an example; it was important for me. This was when I was doing my dissertation. I was reading from the field of literary criticism. I drew from that field because they were into the notion of context. This was in the late 1970s, early 1980s. That lead to my dissertation, which leads to thinking about the context where kids were operating when we were working with them one on one. I was trying to see what was relevant.
>
> One thing I do have, we mentioned before, is the communities of practice book; I found that really important. I was looking at Wenger's book through the work with the districts. It is important to have a combination; that is why I go out and do these interviews with MIST (Middle-School Mathematics and the Institutional Setting of Teaching project) and so on so that I can have teachers, classrooms, and schools to think with as I read stuff.

Dr. Barufaldi said the same thing. He also pointed out to do research; he studies various things. He gave an example of what he was reading as a science educator:

> I think the new science educators must be divergent in their readings. I was thinking about when we were growing up in science education, we did not read anything other than science education type articles. We never went into ed psychology; they thought cognitive psychologist were pseudoscientists. They did not put any faith or confidences in educational psychologists who were talking about things such as learning, thinking.
>
> I just read one article where there were twelve co-authors. It just shows you that even science is done in a collaborative way bringing in all kinds of perspectives. I think it is not just from the scientist point of view, but educators must move in that direction.

> ➤ *Team leaders also surround themselves with other experts to gain knowledge and bounce around ideas.*

Innovative leaders not only read and reflect from experiences, but they also surround themselves with an interdisciplinary community of experts that they can learn from and bounce around ideas with. According to Dr. Barufaldi,

If I were developing a research team right now, I would make sure that there was a cognitive scientist, science and math content specialists, and science educators. That is the kind of team that I would build upon. It is not just a one-person team anymore.

The expertise of the leader is helpful in supporting the team to innovate. The next section will elaborate on the many hats the leader wears to lead a team to make discoveries.

The team leader serves in many capacities depending on the situation. These include being a facilitator, a coach, and a co-learner. The innovative leader's actions are an interplay of these different roles depending on the situation.

EMPOWER OTHERS TO TAKE INITIATIVE

> *An effective leader empowers others.*

Empowerment and ownership have been mentioned several times. When you are given the freedom to create and feel empowered, you are more likely to take risks and be innovative. When work is prescriptive, it leaves little room for creativity and innovation. People need clearly defined roles, but within that role they need the space to create and contribute to the enterprise.

Dr. Cobb was asked what advice he would give to a young scholar who might lead a research team. His advice applies to any discipline as well, not just academia. He pointed out that people skills are necessary. You need to help people focus on tasks and not egos. Part of the problem of egos can be addressed by carefully selecting your team members. Nevertheless, helping focus the goal on the tasks through interaction is important. According to Dr. Cobb,

A lot of what I do, I just do. . . . What I just said, the people you involve in the project, people skills are very important. To the greatest extent possible, it is influencing people so that they are focusing on problems and issues more than themselves. Task involvement and ego involvement, that will be involvement.

The leaders shared their perspectives of how to handle situations when a team member is not a good fit or task oriented. Dr. Barufaldi replied that he never had to ask a member to leave the team, but they eventually exited the team because the rest of the team thought that person was not a good fit. Dr. Mitchell Nathan pointed out they just don't invite people to be part of the team if they felt that person was not a good fit.

> ➢ *Structure and organize things so that everyone has an entry point.*

An interesting point that Dr. Cobb also made is the importance of the leader structuring and organizing things so that all team members regardless of entry point can participate. What this means is that everyone does not have the same level of skills, knowledge, or expertise. However, when you clearly define tasks based on people's interests and skills, you give them an entry point. Dr. Cobb stated,

> I think it is, for example, in your case you go off and lead work with teachers; you are the only person in the room who has been there before, and that should orient you as a leader. You should structure and organize things so that other people who are novices can participate in a pretty substantial way initially, even though they may not know what it looks like.

He talked about individuals who might have academic knowledge but might lack practical experiences, so when they work on his research team, he structures experiences for success:

> You can read words—you can say it—but it is not the same as doing it. You have to play the scaffolding role. The other thing I have to say is you want this group of people to do what you want to do. That is to perform the task.
> Your role should be educative, even on the task of a project. I just gave the example of iterative design. Your job is to organize a structure to support their learning about key ideas and aspects of methodology.

Dr. Franke also talked about structuring experiences so that the whole team can learn. (Note: The book *Conducting Productive Meetings: How to Generate and Communicate Ideas for Innovation* explicitly discusses structuring formal and informal experiences.) Dr. Franke stated:

> So, it is in some way trying to learn from all the people in the research endeavor. It is about how you create a space where all voices are valid and taken up, and used.

SERVE AS A COACH TO PUSH BOUNDARIES OF THINKING

The innovative leader is also a cognitive coach, as illustrated in figure 4.2. What I mean by this is that the innovative leader challenges the boundary of thinking of the novice as well as in his or her thinking. This is a very important part of leading a team to innovate. The leader and team members may have an exchange of flow of ideas from the point of an expert and a novice. I will explain how this exchange mutually transforms both individuals' thinking and leads to further questions. The innovative leader and the novice also play a vital role in innovation.

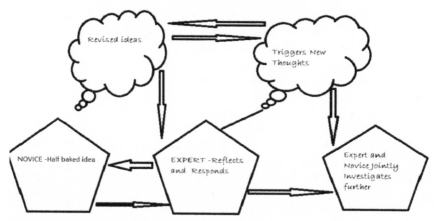

Figure 4.2.   Flow of Ideas between Expert and Novice
Credit: Teruni Lamberg.

For example, when I was part of Dr. Cobb's research team, I noticed that he spent an enormous amount of time listening and responding in writing and verbally to people's ideas. He listened to the thoughts of his team and was open to reflecting on them. He also viewed his role as a demanding and supportive critic to push the novice's thinking. I experienced this process as a postdoc working with Dr. Cobb. Figuring out what worked and what did not work was one way to identify problems to solve according to Dr. Cobb and Dr. Franke. Dr. Cobb stated,

> I just worked in teams. . . . I try to be my own and other people's tough critic. It is meant in a friendly manner. It is a push; it is certainly not an ego thing. It is a push to get the best out of everybody, and I hope to do that for myself as well. I think you are trying to push continually. The other thing I will say . . . I am continuously looking for what is not working.

The point here is that an expert has a different lens than a novice. The interaction between the expert and novice allows for greater discoveries to take place. It is a push between fresh ideas and new lenses of seeing things, testing them against existing knowledge and theories and forging something new.

For example, Dr. Cobb and the rest of the research team were flying back to Nashville after we had collected data. I had been working on organizing the data and created a rough document in which I thought might be some emerging themes. When I looked at the data, I noted some themes that I found interesting.

What I noticed was a "tree in the forest" as a novice and not the entire landscape. I had not situated the tree in the forest to appreciate the novelty of what I was thinking. I passed the sheet of paper to Dr. Cobb; he got excited by what I had jotted down and asked me to investigate things further. He posed questions. We started sharing back and forth talking about what we were seeing and what this meant. The significant point in that conversation was that his expertise could situate the data in the forest. The posing of questions led to asking further questions, which resulted in collecting more data. We had other team members provide input. These discoveries resulted in a paper being published in a prestigious research journal that is now widely cited.

Dr. Cobb could recognize novelty. His thinking may not have been triggered if I had not shared my rough notes with him. This mutual exchange leads to significant research findings. The expert serves as a cognitive coach to push a novice's thinking. However, a novice is not constrained by predetermined thinking and may have the ability to see things in an entirely novel way. The interaction between the expert and novice is mutually beneficial to both. The exchange led to further questions and further refinement of ideas and data collection.

Without the cognitive coaching, I may have noticed something. However, I may not have recognized its novelty or significance. Science is the ability to see things that already exist in novel ways. The interaction was mutually beneficial for learning for both of us. A novice plays an interesting role because prior knowledge and structures do not constrain them. The expert can recognize it in different ways.

There are some important points that you can think about. If you have people in your team who are novices and lack the particular expertise you may have, these people still can provide valuable insights to challenge your thinking. They may notice things, but not recognize the significance of novelty due to lack of experience or knowledge. By having a synergistic relationship, great ideas can emerge. This creates conditions for innovation and discoveries.

What I described is like the theory of cognitive apprenticeship that was developed by Collins, Brown, and Newman; the expert provides coaching, scaffolds the novice's thinking, and has the novice compare their thinking to the expert's and others' thinking.[10] The novice further explores the problem. If you are in academia, this interaction has implications for how you work with postdocs and graduate students. You don't have to be in academia to have these kinds of experiences.

BE A CO-LEARNER

> *Team members interact with equal power and build on each other's ideas.*

The leader is also a co-learner in other situations. This means when the team interacts to discuss ideas, the leader is a co-learner and does not act as the expert, but rather learns from the expertise of the team. The team was put together because of members' unique background. Therefore, it is important to capitalize on the teams' expertise and value what everyone brings.

The leader may have certain expertise. However, when meeting with the team, it is important to recognize that other team members bring knowledge and skills that the leader does not have. This puts the team members in the position of experts and the team leader in the learner position. Many of the people I interviewed emphasized how important it was to play this role.

It is not the leader prescribing, commanding, and telling the team what to think and do. Rather, the team leader is a listener, a co-learner, and on equal footing with the rest of the team. This creates a nonthreatening environment to share ideas, as discussed earlier. Dr. Gutiérrez shared with me that she treats her research team as "colleagues," as opposed to the professor who is in charge and graduate students who follow:

> My research teams operate more like colleagues brainstorming together rather than a professor and grad students. When we code, my students often convince me that something should be coded this way that I had not thought of; it does not come down that I make all the decisions. I end up learning as much from them as they learn from me. This goes back to the idea of the lenses that we all bring to this process of doing research. I already have my lenses and if I am the only one directing things, the project will be limited. It's like looking with only my eyes.

Figuring out a problem together by building on each other's ideas is another way to become a learning community. The leader structures the problem or has the group define the problem to solve. Dr. Franke shared her experience running a research team meeting. She talked about learning new ideas from her graduate students:

> The same would be in any research project I work on. I would not be using sociocultural theory in the same way without my graduate students. I would not know about critical race theory the same way. The ways that I know and the ways that my doctoral students *open up spaces*, where it is not about what I say and do.
>
> It is about what we all figured out together. Their voices and ideas get put on the table, and recognized in the sense that they are all going to have different expertise, and different ideas to bring to the table.
>
> Not everyone has to have an idea at the same time, and just because someone has one now does not mean that they won't have one later. There is an opportunity for people to get excited by each other's ideas and learn in ways that *build the work*.
>
> Instead of everyone off working on their own thing, or taking it in a different direction, we pull those ideas together in ways that they can leverage each other so that the *ideas build on each other*.

Therefore, ensuring that the team understands what unique perspective each team member brings to the project is important. There should be an equal platform for everyone to contribute. It does not matter about the education or background because each person has something important to contribute.

CHAPTER SUMMARY

Create conditions for creative flow of ideas.
Team members feel empowered to take risks and generate ideas.

The leader plays a crucial role in setting the tone and creating the conditions for creativity. This process involves making sure that team members feel valued and supported. Leadership skills should be refined over time. Mindfulness is one way to ensure that the leader is thinking about what he or she is doing and the impact it has on others. The leader must be a lifelong learner and gain expertise.

Expert knowledge helps the leader support team members to innovate. The expert knowledge can be acquired through lived experiences, reading within and across disciplines, and interaction with experts. The leader wears many hats depending on the situation to push the leader's as well as the team members' boundaries of thinking for innovation.

This role involves serving as a facilitator by structuring experiences that allow all team members to have entry points and contribute. The interaction as a cognitive coach is valuable. The third aspect is that the leader is a learner and learns from the expertise of teammates. The team functions as colleagues as opposed to a hierarchical relationship.

STRATEGIES FOR CREATING OPTIMAL
CONDITIONS TO GENERATE IDEAS

Attitude Matters

- Have a positive and supportive attitude.
- The team leader cares about the team members as individuals.
- The leader thinks positively and has an abundant mentality to ensure that the team members benefit from participating in the team.

Leadership Skills Needed to Support a Creative Flow of Ideas

- Innovative leaders are lifelong learners.
- Innovative leaders develop expertise. (See table 4.1.)

Table 4.1. Kinds of Knowledge and Experiences Innovative Leaders Develop

Kinds of Knowledge	Affordances
Research of literature within discipline	Has strong knowledge base
Interdisciplinary perspective, literature within other disciplines	Allows for panoramic or 360-degree view of things to make connections
Real-world experiences	Has experiences to draw from to make sense of what is learned and read

Credit: Teruni Lamberg.

Strategies on How to Create Conditions for Creative Flows of Ideas

Note: As a team leader, you need to adapt your role so that it makes sense to facilitate a creative flow of ideas. Sometimes you are structuring activities so that the team can participate, at times you act as the expert to challenge the thinking of team members, and at other times you become a co-learner and learn from the team. Think about what you are trying to accomplish and what makes sense at that moment.

- Empower others.
- Support team members to focus on tasks, not egos.
- Structure and organize things so that everyone has an entry point.
- Be a co-learner: *learn from the expertise of the team.*
- Serve as a coach to push boundaries of thinking.

Expert/Novice Interaction

- A novice sees something and thinks it is interesting but does not see the "big picture," shares ideas in rough form.
- An expert recognizes the novelty, provides feedback, and poses further questions for their own self-reflection as well as the novice's thinking.
- Multiple communication interactions take place, and each interaction results in an iteration of the idea that is refined.
- The synergistic interaction between the novice and expert leads to new insights. The new insights might lead to further investigations.
- The feedback is immediate, specific, and timely; the specificity is at a very narrow level that pushes the thinking forward for innovation.

NOTES

1. Mihaly Csikszentmihalyi, *Flow and the Psychology of Discovery and Invention* (New York: HarperCollins, 1996).

2. Charles J. Palus and David M. Horth, "Leading Creatively: The Art of Making Sense," *Journal of Aesthetic Education* 30, no. 4 (1996): 53–68.

3. Howard Gardner and Emma Laskin, *Leading Minds: An Anatomy of Leadership* (New York: Basic Books, 2011).

4. Louis Baron, "Authentic Leadership and Mindfulness Development through Action Learning," *Journal of Managerial Psychology* 31, no. 1 (2016): 296–311, https://doi.org/10.1108/JMP-04-2014-0135.

5. Adam Perlman, "Informed Mindfulness as the Foundation for Leadership," *Explore: The Journal of Science and Healing* 11, no. 4 (2015): 324–25.

6. Whitney L. Heppner and Michael H. Kernis, "'Quiet Ego' Functioning: The Complementary Roles of Mindfulness, Authenticity, and Secure High Self-Esteem," *Psychological Inquiry* 18, no. 4 (2007): 248–51.

7. National Research Council, *How People Learn: Brain, Mind, Experience, and School*, expanded ed. (Washington, DC: National Academies Press, 2000).

8. Leo Lionni, *Fish Is Fish* (New York: Random House, 2015).

9. Victoria R. Jacobs, Lisa L. C. Lamb, and Randolph A. Philipp, "Professional Noticing of Children's Mathematical Thinking," *Journal for Research in Mathematics Education* (2010): 169–202.

10. Allan Collins, John Seely Brown, and Susan E. Newman, "Cognitive Apprenticeship: Teaching the Craft of Reading, Writing and Mathematics," *Thinking: The Journal of Philosophy for Children* 8, no. 1 (1988): 2–10.

FIVE

Moving Forward

Wherever you go, go with all your heart!

—Confucius

Leading a team to innovate involves identifying and addressing a real issue or problem that needs to serve a need. Innovation is useful only if it solves real problems and improves things. Therefore, carefully identify the problem from an interdisciplinary perspective. Having an interdisciplinary team is helpful. The innovative leaders pointed out that carefully choosing team members is critical for a highly productive team. The team must be able to work collaboratively together to accomplish things and innovate.

A leader must have a vision and passion for motivating the team. The leader must jointly co-create vision with the team to get a shared understanding. Matching expertise to the project and adapting the project to expertise creates optimal conditions for motivation and creativity. Motivating a team member to participate fully in the project involves considering individual needs and professional and personal benefits. Relationships matter!

Understanding the creative process and how to create conditions to innovate is an important part of leading a team for extraordinary results. The leaders' knowledge and experiences and ability to capitalize on team expertise are necessary. Many of us do not start out to be a leader. However, leadership skills are needed to make a real difference in the lives of others and improve the human condition regardless of discipline.

Leading a team to innovate is different than being a manager. The biggest difference in leading a team to innovate involves generating new ideas and coming up with innovative theories, products, or services to make life a little better for others. Leading to innovate is different than just maintaining the status quo to keep things running.

DESIGN PROJECT MEETINGS FOR CREATIVE PROBLEM-SOLVING

Once a team is assembled to solve a problem, consider how to structure activities to engage the team in creative problem-solving that capitalizes on team expertise. The book *Conducting Productive Meetings: How to Generate and Communicate Ideas for Innovation* provides concrete strategies. The book outlines how to run effective meetings to create and refine ideas to innovate by considering the end user's needs when testing and improving the design. Furthermore, the book emphasizes that effective communication with the team and stakeholders is critical to the project's success.

Consider specifically how to become an intellectual community and engage in the creative process. Understanding the creative process and how to lead meetings that address the creative process is important. Informal and structured activities provide different kinds of opportunities to generate and refine ideas.

MEETINGS SHOULD MOVE PROJECT IDEAS FORWARD

Meetings should drive ideas and the project agenda forward. An organic approach to meetings leads to more creative ideas. The book *Conducting Productive Meetings: How to Generate and Communicate Ideas for Innovation* outlines a "Three Levels of Sense-Making Framework" for running project meetings. This framework incorporates strategies for making thinking explicit, analyzing and building on each other's thoughts, and coming up with shared ideas to move the agenda forward.

The end user's/customer's perspective and feedback during the design process must be considered. Furthermore, the leader can engage in provocative thinking by leveraging resources creatively to solve the problem. The project team and stakeholders might have access to resources to support the work of the team. The book outlines how different innovative leaders made design decisions.

Finally, communication is critical for making a difference. Mechanisms for communication should be relevant, timely, and useful. Communication must not only be limited to the project team but also must extend to the stakeholders and end users/customers.

LEADING TO INNOVATE INVOLVES CONTINUOUS LEARNING

A leader who leads a team to innovate is a lifelong learner. Howard Gardner's framework from his book *Five Minds for the Future* is helpful in thinking about leadership. In his book, he describes five minds that are needed for the future so that people can have productive personal and professional lives. These include the respectful mind, the disciplined mind, the synthesizing mind, the creating mind, and the ethical mind.[1]

Leading a team to innovate involves the intersection of these minds in two ways: The leader needs to develop the five minds of the future within to be effective. The leaders also must create conditions for the team to develop and capitalize on the five minds of the future.

➤ *An ethical mind leads to a higher purpose.*

Dr. Gardner shares that the ethical mind strives to do good work and engage in good citizenship. The ethical mind is needed to come up with a *higher purpose*. The project team must identify a problem in society and find solutions to make things better. Dr. Gardner points out that this process involves understanding the core values of one's profession. He writes about being a good steward in the face of obstacles and even being willing to speak out at a personal cost to be a good steward.[2] Dr. Jbeily advised that in the "face of obstacles and adversity, you should never change your principles and goals."

➤ *A disciplined mind is needed to think creatively and innovatively.*

Leading a team to innovate requires disciplinary and interdisciplinary knowledge and the ability to continue learning. The project team including the leader needs to have core disciplinary knowledge and an interdisciplinary knowledge. This is because the project team should examine a problem from a 360-degree perspective to come up with creative solutions.

Dr. Gardner points out that people need disciplinary knowledge within a core discipline. Also, they also need the ability to acquire interdisciplinary knowledge and continue learning. He also writes that people need to develop ways of thinking within the core disciplines.

➤ *The synthesizing mind is needed to make sense of information.*

An important part of leading a team to innovate involves making sense of what is happening as the project unfolds. Design work is an important part of innovation. It requires asking questions such as: "What is working?" "What is not working, and why?" Structuring project meetings to focus on ideas and examining what is happening is helpful. This process also involves sifting through a lot of information and identifying key findings related to the project goals. This process includes filtering and refining ideas into essential ideas. Once ideas are refined, the team can make decisions needed to make progress toward project goals.

> ➤ *The creating mind and the respectful mind are needed to communicate with each other, generate ideas, and solve problems.*

The purpose of innovation is to make things better, faster, or cheaper. The "creating minds" and "respectful minds" are needed for innovation. Dr. Gardner points out that individuals need to think beyond existing knowledge in powerful ways.[3] People need to be able to come up with creative solutions that push the boundaries of current knowledge. This is the whole purpose of leading to innovate. Leading to innovate is the ability to improve things and make them better. It also involves coming up with novel solutions.

The leader must structure experiences for the team to create. This process involves a combination of formal and informal experiences. The innovative leader interviews revealed the importance of working *organically* and *flexibly* to solve problems. This process involves engaging in provocative thinking by leveraging resources and solving problems creatively. Productive discussion is necessary to generate ideas, refine ideas, and move toward creative solutions.

The "respectful mind," according to Dr. Gardner, involves the ability to interact with each other in constructive and respectful ways.[4] The leader must cultivate a culture of respect within the team. This part includes valuing and honoring people. Informal experiences allow team members to get to know each other personally. These relationships are important for sharing ideas and tackling challenging and stressful problems. The "respectful mind" should not only apply to how the team interacts with each other. It should extend to the community that the team is serving and all stakeholders. A key theme that emerged from the innovative leader interviews was the desire to make a difference!

VOICES FROM THE FIELD:
INNOVATIVE K–12 LEADER INTERVIEWS

How to Build an Action Plan

This section contains interviews with K–12 innovative leaders. Their work has made a significant impact in their respective communities. The interviews reflect experiences and insights gained by these leaders in the field. The principles outlined in this book can be used in any setting to lead a team to solve a problem and innovate, not just in education. The interviews represent just one context.

Find Your Higher Purpose and Figure Out Your Agenda

Finding your higher purpose motivates you to act!

Lamberg: How did you build an action plan by connecting to your higher purpose?

INTERVIEW WITH MS. DENISE TRAKAS, K–12 COORDINATOR, WASHOE COUNTY SCHOOL DISTRICT, RENO, NEVADA

> *Figure out passion and move forward even when there is uncertainty!*

The first day I walked into my new classroom I looked around at all the faces, the small hands, the eager movements, and I saw promise and possibility. I wasn't sure what I needed to do or how I was going to do it. But I knew that I needed to do everything I could to open up future opportunities for my students. I had to visualize needs I could barely understand myself. I had to keep reminding myself that the curriculum and standards were just the foundation for something much greater and opened my mind to that unknowingness.

INTERVIEW WITH MR. DAVID EBERT, OREGON HIGH SCHOOL MATH TEACHER / LEADERSHIP TEAM, OREGON, WISCONSIN, NCTM BOARD MEMBER

> *Asking the question "Why?" helps connect higher purpose and actions when making structural changes.*

In one sense, having a group of educators connect to a higher purpose is easy, because all good teachers and administrators have students at the center of their decision-making processes. In another sense, however, connecting to a higher purpose is very difficult, because it is easy to focus on structural changes in education, and these easy fixes often have very little impact on student achievement. For example, changing a school's schedule will have little to no impact on student achievement unless comprehensive changes are also made to the way our teachers teach, and our students learn.

In our school's leadership team, we constantly remind ourselves to start with "why?" When our conversations turn to structural changes we can try in our school, we remind ourselves to look at the bigger picture and keep student learning at the forefront of everything we do. We need a significant reason why we should consider a change before we consider the "what" and "how" of the change.

INTERVIEW WITH MARISSA MCCLISH, STUDENT LEARNING OBJECTIVE COORDINATOR, WASHOE SCHOOL DISTRICT, RENO, NEVADA

> *The "aha" insights from a current work position become a mantra to guide work.*

I had some "aha" moments in every position that I have had and left with some major mantras. One related to my current work is that I believe that high-stakes assessments of what happens every day. When I have "aha moment" as a mantra, I follow them as the value of the job. I repeat things that we are doing as a team and provide visibility into my belief system and value in the work to have a shared philosophy. This helps the team put their own passion and values into the work that they are doing. It's interesting to hear something they repeat on the spot spontaneously that is something new or novel and they link that to the work they brought in as a group. It is very cool to see people who work with a shared philosophy for the betterment of the team and the team grows when we are passionate.

INTERVIEW WITH MS. HOLLY MARICH, REGIONAL TRAINER, NORTHEASTERN NEVADA PROFESSIONAL DEVELOPMENT PROGRAM, ELY, NEVADA

> *Take the initiative, take risks, and invest in what you believe in!*

Leadership opportunities started coming my way once I was recognized as a leader at my school. These opportunities came from both my administrator and my own initiative and willingness to volunteer. For example, I was asked by my principal to participate with a state-level committee revising state standards. Other opportunities I experienced were from noticing the opportunity and volunteering to help. I would also take the initiative to invest in myself and in my classroom to better teach the way I wanted to teach. When I asked my school for tables rather than desks in my classroom to better support a collaborative teaching and learning environment, my request was denied.

Because the learning environment was so important to me, I chose to use my own money to purchase tables for my classroom. I also believed attending professional conferences was a worthwhile investment in my learning. Therefore, I paid my own way to attend national conferences like the International Reading Association (IRA; now the International Literacy Association, ILA). My first year of teaching, I knew I wanted to attend the IRA conference. At the time, my district did not value conference attendance as professional development. I had to go before the school board to ask if they would pay for my substitute while I would cover my own travel and conference expenses. After attending the conference, I had to report back to the school board.

I was told that when I talked to the board members about what I had learned at the conference, my passion and energy made an impact. Soon after, the school board started to talk about how important it is for teachers to go to conferences and have these professional development opportunities. I had no idea this would be a consequence of my conference attendance. Even now, well over a decade later, I take for granted how a commitment to my own professional learning influenced a positive change for others.

Reflecting back, I notice how a lot of the work into becoming a leader was me going after what I wanted with my own time and money, all of which I considered a worthy investment in myself as a professional. One significant investment in time was attending six-week summer institute offered each summer by the National Writing Project state affiliates.

I had no idea what the writing project summer institute was. I just knew other educators I admired had said it was such as great experience and teachers that are leaders attend the summer institute. I left my three small children and husband at home for six weeks so I could attend the nearest writing project summer institute in a city 250 miles away from my home. This investment in myself as a teacher and leader has, both then and to this day, provided many important learning and leadership opportunities. One major takeaway from the summer institute was my involvement in teacher inquiry communities, also known as action research. I started facilitating action research groups with teachers in my district. This eventually led to my connection with the Action Research Network of the Americas (ARNA). Similar to my path toward leadership in teaching, I started volunteering with work for ARNA. I am now on the executive committee for ARNA.

HOW TO ASSEMBLE AN INTERDISCIPLINARY
TEAM TO SOLVE A PROBLEM

Develop a Strategic Vision and Assemble a Dream Team

Defining your vision allows you to select your team members strategically.

Lamberg: What problem are you trying to solve? How did you decide on what kind of expertise is needed in your team? What things should people in K–12 settings consider when putting a team together to solve a problem?

INTERVIEW WITH MS. KATHY DEES, PROFESSIONAL DEVELOPMENT COORDINATOR, SOUTHERN NEVADA REGIONAL PROFESSIONAL DEVELOPMENT PROGRAM, LAS VEGAS, NEVADA

➤ *Purposeful work and consistency are needed to get buy-in!*

Our professional development group is often called upon to work with schools to increase student engagement and content knowledge in mathematics. Our first step is to work with the leadership team onsite. Depending upon the funding that schools have, this can also include coaches. The central idea of making change happen is buy-in from the participants, consistency with the professional development, and follow up by the leadership team. To make this happen the school needs to see the professional development as purposeful. Once the process starts, it's always critical to look for leaders within the school to create a buzz and be an available resource. The sustainability in the change comes from the teachers and their willingness to move forward with implementation and refinement.

INTERVIEW WITH MR. DAVID EBERT, OREGON HIGH SCHOOL MATH TEACHER/ LEADERSHIP TEAM, OREGON, WISCONSIN, NCTM BOARD MEMBER

> *Selecting people with a common vision and passion and working together transforms the group into a community of practice.*

I recently formed a team of teachers to be the program committee for the Wisconsin Mathematics Council (WMC) annual conference. These volunteers would be responsible for every aspect of building the schedule for the conference—the WMC's biggest undertaking of the year. I sought advice from others to help build the team.

We looked for people from schools that were doing innovative things, and also looked to have representation from all levels of K–12.

We selected people who share our common vision to host the best state-level math conference in the country, are passionate about improving math education for all students, have a positive attitude and a growth mindset, and are potential future leaders in the WMC. Everyone who was asked to join the committee accepted the invitation, and we have worked together to build the program for two conferences. During this time, we have transformed from a committee to a community of practice, and every member of our group has stepped up to take the lead on a certain aspect of the conference planning.

INTERVIEW WITH MS. JILL ROSS, PRINCIPAL, ALPINE ACADEMY PREP HIGH SCHOOL

> *Selecting the right people and setting clear expectations is important!*

We bring on team members who are hardworking and humble. We then communicate with all teachers the importance of creating a love of learning in their classrooms! We encourage them to provide a warm welcome feel in the class, develop engaging lessons, and keep the expectations high. We focus on a growth mindset. We explain to teachers and students that it is okay to take risks, experience failure, and work hard. We feel like we have created a place where teachers and students enjoy each day of learning.

HOW TO CAPITALIZE ON TEAM EXPERTISE

Create a Blueprint for Success!

The team can function because they know their larger purpose and individual contributions.

Lamberg: How did you communicate your vision to your team and get buy-in? What was the process to ensure that everyone knew what they were expected to do?

INTERVIEW WITH MR. DAVID EBERT, OREGON HIGH SCHOOL MATH TEACHER / LEADERSHIP TEAM, OREGON, WISCONSIN, NCTM BOARD MEMBER

➤ *Focusing on mission and vision helps keep conversations focused on goals!*

I served on the board of directors of the Wisconsin Mathematics Council for many years. Our board brought together people of diverse backgrounds from across the state. Our organization's mission and vision were printed on the back of our name tents, so they were visible to us throughout our meetings. When we had dialogues and planning, we would remind ourselves to come back to our mission and vision, which focused our work. As leaders, we passionately believe in the mission and vision, and keep it at the center of all we do.

INTERVIEW WITH MS. KATHY DEES, PROFESSIONAL DEVELOPMENT COORDINATOR, SOUTHERN NEVADA REGIONAL PROFESSIONAL DEVELOPMENT PROGRAM, LAS VEGAS, NEVADA

➤ *Collective planning leads to more engagement and buy-in.*

I have had experience being part of planning teams that have been led with both a top-down and a collective approach. When the team plans under inflexible leadership with the top-down approach, many dynamics influence the outcome. First, there is limited passion and buy-in from the team when they feel their ideas are not valued. The opportunities for change become limited because different viewpoints are not brought to the table. Secondly, when it becomes time for implementation, the can have a shallow understanding of key ideas and purpose.

When teams plan collectively, there is more engagement and buy-in to the process. One structure I have experienced is when the facilitator of the group generates ideas from the team about the end goal and records them. Instead of trying to discuss/plan each idea, the facilitator has the individuals in the group choose which idea they want to dig into further. When these smaller focus groups meet, the idea is discussed in more detail, which leads to more diversity of solutions. The subgroups meet back together and create a final cohesive plan. This structure allows the participant to be the expert on the idea they choose, but still have input on all aspects of the final outcome. When they are asked to share the plan, they are more knowledgeable and passionate.

K–12 INNOVATIVE LEADER BIOGRAPHIES

Ms. Kathy Dees, *Southern Nevada Regional Professional Development coordinator, Las Vegas*

Kathy Dees's career in education began in Clark County School District (CCSD) in Las Vegas, Nevada, teaching second, third, and fourth grade. During her time in the district she worked as a project facilitator for the Math and Science Enhancement Project (MASE), which was funded by the National Science Foundation (NSF). This grant provided the funding for ongoing professional development to select schools in CCSD to deepen K–5 science and math education reform.

Kathy Dees currently works as a project facilitator for Southern Nevada Regional Development Program (SNRPDP), which provides professional development to the five southern counties in Nevada. Kathy's focus in professional development with the teachers includes math practices and content to enhance the teachers' practice with the result being student understanding. Kathy's curiosity about finding ways to make math meaningful for students drove her to make a difference. She encourages students to pose questions and experience "aha" moments in mathematics. Working for SNRPDP gives her the opportunity to support teachers in their own math practice.

Mr. David Ebert, *high school math teacher/leadership team member/NCTM board member, Oregon, Wisconsin*

Mr. Ebert is a mathematics teacher at Oregon High School in southern Wisconsin, and a member of his school's leadership team. He has been teaching students in grades 6–12 for over twenty years. He is the past president of the Wisconsin Mathematics Council and serves on the board of directors of the National Council of Teachers of Mathematics, and has held multiple leadership roles in both organizations. He has led workshops for teachers on a variety of topics at the local, state, and national level. He is a past recipient of a Kohl Fellowship, the Marquette University School of Education Young Alumnus of the Year Award, a Best Buy Teach Award, and the Miriam Connellan Mathematics Education Award. He was recently honored as a Wisconsin Mathematics Council Distinguished Mathematics Educator.

Ms. Holly Marich, *Professional Development regional coordinator, Northeastern Nevada Regional Professional Development Program, Ely, Nevada*

Over the past twenty-three years, Holly has been an educator in many capacities: a parent-volunteer, substitute teacher, summer school teacher, and full-time elementary school teacher. She is currently a regional coordinator at the Northeastern Nevada Regional Professional Development Program in Nevada. She works with teachers across the Northeastern region of the state around topics of literacy and technology. She is also currently a Ph.D. candidate at Michigan State University in the educational psychology and educational technology (EPET) hybrid program.

In addition to her work at MSU, Holly serves on the executive committee as director of membership for the Action Research Network of the Americas. She has won numerous awards, including the Literacy Research Association's Dissertation Proposal Mentoring Pre-Conference Program, White Pine County School District Elk's Teacher of the Month, the Vietnam Fellowship to Enhance Global Awareness (Michigan State University College of Education), the Nevada Association of School Boards Innovative Teacher of the Year (2011), and Lincoln Highway Historical Society Teacher of the Year 2005.

Ms. Marissa McClish, student learning objective coordinator, Washoe School District, Reno, Nevada

Marissa taught high school math and science in Ann Arbor, Michigan, and San Francisco, California, prior to working outside of the classroom in northern Nevada. In Nevada, she helped launch a school-wide STEM program while serving as a middle school instructional coach and has served as regional educational trainer in six school districts. Her primary passion and work outside of the classroom has focused on accessibility of quality instruction for all students and empowering teachers to bring engaging, student-driven pedagogy to their classrooms.

Marissa holds a B.S. in engineering in atmospheric, oceanic, and space sciences and a M.Ed. in curriculum and instruction. She is currently working as a district administrator in the Washoe County School District Department of Assessment. Marissa has been active in math circles and is currently serving as co-president of the Northern Nevada Math Council. She has spoken at national meetings for the National Council of Teachers of Math and Student Achievement Partners. She continues to be driven by the belief that education is the most complex profession out there and to be inspired by the continual learning that the field offers.

Ms. Jill Ross, principal, Alpine Academy College Prep High School, Sparks, Nevada

Ms. Ross is the principal of Alpine Academy College Prep High School, located in Sparks, Nevada. She, along with the vice principal, are the original founders. Mrs. Ross started her education career in a small charter school as a social studies and health teacher. She then taught in the local district while she earned her master's in education administration and supervision. Next, she worked as an instructional coach in the district before opening Alpine Academy in 2009. Her school's growth from a 42 percent graduation rate its first year to a 100 percent graduation rate by year five was accomplished with an outstanding team. Mrs. Ross was awarded the Charter School Principal of the Year Award in 2015 and attributed it to a positive culture and strong work ethic at Alpine Academy.

Ms. Denise Trakas, *program coordinator of math curriculum, Washoe County School District, Nevada*

Ms. Trakas is the program coordinator of math curriculum in Washoe County School District, Reno, Nevada. Before that, she served as a regional trainer in the Northwestern Regional Professional Development Program. She also taught elementary school prior to taking on leadership positions. Her work has included supporting state-approved, district-adopted instructional resources, and developing student and family support for the curriculum. Also, she oversees outreach and collaboration with the state of Nevada, Nevada institutions of higher education, and national mathematics collaborations and partnerships. She was recently awarded the Dream Box Learning Hero Award, which is a national award. Ms. Trakas serves on the board of many national committees such as NCSM, NCTM, and on the board of the Northern Nevada Mathematics Council.

INNOVATIVE LEADER BIOGRAPHIES

James Barufaldi, Ph.D.

Professor emeritus, former director, Center for STEM Education, the University of Texas at Austin, a consultant on developing partnerships and STEM education, Dr. James P. Barufaldi was the Ruben E. Hinojosa Regents Professor at the University of Texas at Austin and served as the director of the Center for STEM Education. He also served as principal investigator of the Texas Regional Collaboratives for Excellence in Science Teaching. He served as co-director of the Teach Secondary Science and Mathematics Teacher Preparation Program. He has supervised more than sixty dissertations and theses in science education.

Dr. Barufaldi was instrumental in developing STEM education at the University of Texas and has an impressive record of scholarship. He directed numerous federally funded projects such as the U.S. Department of Education Project—General Science Content and Inquiry Skills Improvement Program, the Title II–funded Coordinated Thematic Science In-Service Program, the Science Content Improvement Program, the Texas Elementary Science In-Service Program, and the NSF project ESTT (Empower Science Teachers of Texas). Dr. Barufaldi's research program involved areas of professional development, curriculum design, instructional strategies, and science education. He is known for building strong collaborations within the education community in Texas.

Dr. Barufaldi was selected as a member of the Academy of Distinguished Teachers at the University of Texas at Austin in 2003. He was named a Minnie Stevens Piper Professor, 2002, for "dedication to the teaching profession" as well as "outstanding academic, scientific, and scholarly achievement." He served as president of the National Association for Research in Science Teaching, among others. He also received the 2002 Outstanding Scholar in Education Award presented by the Alumni Association, College of Education, at the University of Maryland, College Park, and received an honorary doctor of science degree from Marietta College (Ohio) and the Texas Excellence Teaching Award in the College of Education at the University of Texas.

Currently, he is active internationally as a STEM consultant and is investigating the process of building successful collaboratives in the global STEM education community, including variables that may contribute to high-intensity, sustained collaboration.

Paul Cobb, Ph.D.

Dr. Paul Cobb is a renowned professor in mathematics education at Vanderbilt University. He was awarded the Joe B. Wyatt Distinguished University Professor at Vanderbilt University. His work has earned him numerous awards and honors.

These award and honors include the Sir Alan Newell Visiting Fellowship, Griffith University, Brisbane, Australia. He was inducted to the National Academies and is a member. He is also an invited fellow of the Center for Advanced Studies in the Behavioral Sciences.

Dr. Cobb was awarded the Hans Freudenthal Medal for cumulative research program over the prior ten years from the International Commission on Mathematics Instruction in 2005. He is a founding class member at the American Education Research Association (AERA).

He won the University of Georgia College of Education Lifetime Achievement Alumni Award, and the Sylvia Scribner Award for a program of work conducted within ten years that represents a significant advancement in our understanding of learning and instruction (2010). He was recently awarded the honor of a distinguished scholar at the AERA Special Interest Group for Research in Mathematics Education.

Dr. Cobb has served as a principal investigator on numerous grants. His research interests focus on instructional design, issues of equity in mathematics teaching and learning, and the improvement of mathematics teaching on a large scale. Dr. Cobb's current research examines making instructional improvement of mathematics at scale.

A book edited by Erna Yackel, Koeno Gravemeijer, and Anna Sfard that describes the evolution of his research program was published in 2010: *A Journey in Mathematics Education Research: Insights from the Research of Paul Cobb*. He is a coeditor of *Improving Access to Mathematics: Diversity and Equity in the Classroom* and *Symbolizing and Communicating in Mathematics Classrooms: Perspectives on Discourse, Tools and Instructional Design*. In addition, he coedited *The Emergence of Mathematical Meaning: Interaction in Classroom Cultures* with Heinrich Bauersfeld.

Robert Chang, Ph.D.

Dr. Robert Chang is the director of the Materials Research Institute at Northwestern University. He is a professor of materials science and engineering. His research focuses on unconventional solar cell design, fabrication, and analysis, nanostructured carbon tubes and molecules, photonic crystals, amorphous semiconducting oxide films, and nanostructured plasmonic materials in the infrared.

He has an impressive track record of accomplishments. He served as the president of the Materials Research Society (MRS) in 1989; fellow, 2008; Woody Award, 1987; councilor, 1986–1988. He was an honorary member of materials research societies of India, Japan, and Korea. He was a Siu Lien Ling Wong Fellow, the Chinese University of Hong Kong, 1999, and a fellow of the American Vacuum Society.

He received the NSF Director's Distinguished Teaching Scholar Award in 2005. He has served as a member of the International Advisory Board of NIMS, Japan; a member of the "Visionary Board" of MINATEC, CEA, France; and general secretary and founding president of International Union of Material Research Societies (IUMRS).

Dr. Chang is a visionary leader who has made significant discoveries not just in the sciences. His center developed Materials World Modules (MWM). These are hands-on, inquiry- and design-based curriculum units for middle and high school students. These units are based on materials science and nanotechnology principles. It uses an interdisciplinary approach to engage students and has proven to increase science knowledge and student interest. His vision is to engage young students' minds.

Megan Franke, Ph.D.

Dr. Megan Franke is an education professor at the Graduate School of Education and Information Studies (GSE&IS) at UCLA. Dr. Franke has served as director of UCLA's Center X from 2001 to 2008, chair of the

UCLA Department of Education from 2008 to 2013, and interim dean of GSE&IS in 2012.

She has won numerous awards and has been recognized for her work. She was recently appointed to the National Academies. Dr. Franke, along with her colleagues, was honored with the AERA Henry T. Truba Award for Research Leading to the Transformation of the Social Context in Education along with AERA's Relating Research to Practice Award. She serves as a member at large at the AERA Council and a member of the AERA Executive Board.

Dr. Franke's research focuses on understanding and supporting teacher learning for both preservice and in-service teachers. She studies how teaching mathematics with attention to students and their mathematical thinking can create opportunities for low-income students of color to learn mathematics with understanding. She is known for her leadership in Center X: Where Research and Practice Intersect for Urban School Professionals and her ongoing professional development work to support teachers, schools, and communities.

Dr. Franke has coauthored several books: *Children's Mathematics: Cognitively Guided Instruction; Young Children's Mathematics: Cognitively Guided Instruction in Early Childhood Education;* and *Thinking Mathematics: Integrating Arithmetic & Algebra in Elementary School.*

Rochelle Gutierrez, Ph.D.

Dr. Gutiérrez is a professor of curriculum and instruction and Latina / Latino studies at the University at Illinois at Urbana-Champaign. She has won numerous awards for her work in social justice in mathematics education. She has earned the Excellence in Research Award from the Association of Mathematics Teacher Educators for the work she has conducted and the theories on equity she has offered to the field.

Pace University recognized her as a Distinguished Educator in the Pedagogy of Success in Urban Schools, and TODOS Mathematics for All recently awarded her the Iris M. Carl Equity and Leadership Award. Her work has been published in such journals as *American Educational Research Journal, Mathematical Thinking and Learning, Journal for Research in Mathematics Education, Harvard Educational Review, Democracy and Education, Urban Review,* and *Mathematics Teacher.*

She has served as a member of the writing team for the Standards for Preparing Teachers of Mathematics produced by the Association of Mathematics Teacher Educators. On a Fulbright fellowship, she studied secondary mathematics teachers in Zacatecas, México, where she was able to document the different cultural practices and algorithms used in Mexican classrooms.

Dr. Gutierrez's research interrogates the unearned privilege that mathematics holds in society and the roles that race, class, language, and gender play in teaching and learning mathematics so as to open up a new possible relationship between living beings, mathematics, and the planet.

Her current research projects include: theorizing the roles of mathematics in relation to power, identity, the body, and authority in society; supporting mathematics teachers who engage their students in rigorous and creative mathematics and who are committed to social justice; and documenting moments of "Nepantla" and "creative insubordination" in the everyday practices of mathematics teachers. She is writing a book called *The Mirror Test*.

Kamil A. Jbeily, Ph.D.

Dr. Kamil A. Jbeily is currently president of Reach the Stars Enterprise: Leadership, Partnerships, and Systemic Reform. Dr. Jbeily was born in Beirut, Lebanon. Completing a B.S. in chemistry and masters of science in chemistry and chemistry education, Kamil taught in the Lebanese secondary schools. In 1980, he immigrated to the United States to attend the University of Texas at Austin, where he earned his Ph.D. in science education.

In 1986, Dr. Jbeily joined the Texas Education Agency (TEA), first as a science specialist, then as director of science projects. In 1991, Kamil founded the Texas Regional Collaboratives for Excellence in Science and Mathematics Teaching (TRC). Under his leadership, this joint initiative of TEA, University of Texas–Austin, and multiple corporations, grew into a dynamic, statewide network of P–16 partnerships that has improved the knowledge, skills, and performance of over fifty thousand teachers of science and mathematics, and benefited the learning of over 3 million students.

Dr. Jbeily founded the TRC based a statewide need to improve science education. He did this by initiating a series of regional meetings across the state to explore ways to create support systems of professional development for Texas science teachers. The meetings included representatives from education service centers, colleges and universities, school districts, business and industry, and institutions of informal education.

The goal was to create regional partnerships built on collaboration and cost-sharing that provided science teachers with relevant, sustained, and high-intensity professional development. These P–16 partnerships, with initial federal funding from the Dwight D. Eisenhower Science Professional Development Program, developed into the statewide network that is now the TRC.

This program won numerous awards. In 2000, Dr. Jbeily was inducted into the Texas Science Hall of Fame, and the governor, the Senate, and the House of Representatives recognized the program for its distinguished achievements and contributions to supporting educational reform.

Dr. Jbeily has always been an active educator. He has never lost touch with the classroom; he served as an adjunct professor of chemistry at Austin Community College from 1985 until 2015. Also, he is a sought-after motivational speaker, having made over two hundred presentations in the United States and internationally on leadership, excellence, equity, diversity, systemic reform, and founding and sustaining partnerships.

H. Richard Milner IV, Ph.D.

H. Richard Milner IV is the Helen Faison Endowed Chair of Urban Education, professor of education, as well as the director of the Center for Urban Education at the University of Pittsburgh. Dr. Milner is a fellow of the AERA and the recipient of the National Association of Multicultural Education's Carl A. Grant Multicultural Research Award.

Recently, he was honored with the John Dewey Award for relating research to practice and the Innovations in Diversity, Teaching, and Teacher Education Award from Division K of the AERA. His research, teaching, and policy interests include urban teacher education, African American literature, and the social context of education. In particular, Dr. Milner's research examines policies and practices that support teacher success in urban schools.

His research has been recognized by the American Association of Colleges for Teacher Education's 2012 Outstanding Book Award and the American Education Studies Association's Critic's Choice Book Award for the widely read book *Start Where You Are but Don't Stay There: Understanding Diversity, Opportunity Gaps, and Teaching in Today's Classrooms* (Harvard Education Press, 2010). His most recent book is *Rac(e)ing to Class: Confronting Poverty and Race in Schools and Classrooms* (Harvard Education Press, 2015).

Mitchell J. Nathan, Ph.D.

Dr. Nathan is a professor of learning science in the Department of Educational Psychology at the University of Wisconsin–Madison (UW–Madison). He is also the director of the Center on Education and Work and the director of the IES Post-doctoral Fellowship Program in Mathematical Thinking, Learning, and Instruction. He holds faculty appointments in the Department of Curriculum and Instruction, the Psychology Department, and the Wisconsin Center for Education Research (WCER).

He is also a member of the University of Wisconsin Cognitive Science Cluster and the Delta Program Steering Committee. He served as the chair of the Learning Sciences Program from 2004 to 2010. Dr. Nathan has an impressive record of external funding and publications. He has garnered over $25 million dollars in funding. He was inducted into the Teaching Academy at the University of Wisconsin in 2014 and received Exceptionality Designation at the Department of Educational Psychology at the University of Wisconsin in 2009.

Some of Dr. Nathan's current affiliations include the National Academy of Sciences (NAS) Space Studies Board; and the National Research Council (NRC) Board of Science Education; the planning committee for "Sharing the Adventure with the Student: Exploring Intersections of NASA Space Science and Education"; the National Academy of Engineering (NAE) Committee on Integrated STEM Education; the Institute for (P–12) Engineering Research and Learning—INSPIRE; the Latin American School for Education, Cognitive and Neural Science, Universidad de Chile; the Universidad de Buenos Aires, ELS International Institute of Neuroscience and Natal—Brazil; the AERA; the American Society of Engineering Education; the Cognitive Science Society; the National Council of Teachers of Mathematics; and the International Society of the Learning Sciences, a professional community of scholars who take an interdisciplinary approach to the study of learning, for which he was a founding officer.

NOTES

1. Howard Gardner, *Five Minds for the Future* (Boston: Harvard Business Review Press, 2009).

2. Gardner, *Five Minds for the Future*.

3. Gardner, *Five Minds for the Future*.

4. Gardner, *Five Minds for the Future*.

Bibliography

Adiar, John. *The Art of Creative Thinking: How to Be Innovative and Develop Great Ideas.* London; Philadelphia: Kogan Page, 2009.

Amabile, Teresa. "Motivating Creativity in Organizations: On Doing What You Love and Loving What You Do." *California Management Review* 40, no. 1 (1997): 55.

Baron, Louis. "Authentic Leadership and Mindfulness Development through Action Learning," *Journal of Managerial Psychology* 31, no. 1 (2016): 296–31, https://doi.org/10.1108/JMP-04-2014-0135.

Baumgartner, Jeffrey. *The Way of the Innovation Master.* Erps-Kwerps, Belgium: JPB Bwiti, 2010.

Biography.com Editors. "Elon Musk." *Biography.com*, 2017. www.biography.com/people/elon-musk-20837159#early-life.

Canfield, Jack, and Janet Switzer. *The Success Principles: How to Get from Where You Are to Where You Want to Be.* New York: HarperCollins, 2005.

Chafkin, Max. *Eccentric Billionaire Elon Musk from Zero to Hero.* Interview of Elon Musk. 2017.

Collins, Allan, John Seely Brown, and Susan E. Newman. "Cognitive Apprenticeship: Teaching the Craft of Reading, Writing and Mathematics." *Thinking: The Journal of Philosophy for Children* 8, no. 1 (1988): 2–10.

Covey, Stephen. *The 7 Habits of Highly Effective People.* New York: Free Press, 2014.

Covey, Stephen R. *The 8th Habit: From Effectiveness to Greatness.* London: Simon and Schuster, 2014.

Csikszentmihalyi, Mihaly. *Flow and the Psychology of Discovery and Invention.* New York: HarperCollins, 1996.

Gardner, Howard. *Five Minds for the Future.* Boston: Harvard Business Review Press, 2009.

Gardner, Howard, and Emma Laskin. *Leading Minds: An Anatomy of Leadership.* New York: Basic Books, 2011.

George, Bill. *Discover Your True North: Become an Authentic Leader.* 2nd ed. Holbrook, NJ: John Wiley and Sons, 2015.

Goleman, Daniel, Richard Boyatzis, and Annie McKee. *Primal Leadership: Unleashing the Power of Emotional Intelligence.* Boston: Harvard Business School, 2013.

Graham-Leviss, Katherine. "The 5 Skills that Innovative Leaders Have in Common." *Harvard Business Review*, 2016. https://hbr.org/2016/12/the-5-skills-that-innovative-leaders-have-in-common.

Guilford, J. P. "Three Faces of Intellect." *American Psychologist* 14, no. 8 (1959): 469–79.

Heppner, Whitney L., and Michael H. Kernis. "'Quiet Ego' Functioning: The Complementary Roles of Mindfulness, Authenticity, and Secure High Self-Esteem." *Psychological Inquiry* 18, no. 4 (2007): 248–51.

Horth, David Magellan, and D. Buchner. *White Paper on Innovative Leadership: How to Use Innovation to Lead Effectively, Work Collaboratively and Drive Results.* 2015. www.ccl.org/wp-content/uploads/2015/04/InnovationLeadership.pdf.

Horth, David Magellan, and Jonathan Vehar. "Becoming a Leader Who Fosters Innovation." 2014. www.ccl.org/wpcontent/uploads/2014/03/BecomingLeaderFostersInnovation.pdf.

Jacobs, Victoria R., Lisa L. C. Lamb, and Randolph A. Philipp. "Professional Noticing of Children's Mathematical Thinking." *Journal for Research in Mathematics Education* (2010): 169–202.

Katzenbach, Jon, and Douglas Smith. *The Wisdom of Teams: Creating the High-Performance Organizations.* Boston: Harvard Business Review Press, 1993.

Kaufman, Sibyl. "STEM Teaching: Retiring Not Retiring." University of Texas Education Magazine, 2015.

Kelly, Tom. *The Art of Innovation: Lessons in Creativity from IDEO America's Leading Design Firm.* New York: Doubleday, 2007.

Kotter, John P. *Leading Change.* Boston: Harvard Business Review Press, 2012.

Kouzes, James, and Barry Posner. *Leadership Challenge: How to Make Extraordinary Things Happen in Organizations.* 5th ed. San Francisco: Jossey-Bass, 2012.

Lamberg, Teruni. *Conducting Successful Meetings: How to Generate and Communicate Ideas for Innovation.* Lanham, MD: Rowman & Littlefield, 2018.

Lencioni, Patrick. *The Five Dysfunctions of a Team: A Leadership Fable.* San Francisco: Jossey-Bass, 2002.

Lionni, Leo. *Fish Is Fish.* New York: Random House, 2015.

Maxwell, John. *21 Irrefutable Laws of Leadership: Follow Them and People Will Follow You.* Nashville, TN: Thomas Nelson, 2007.

McInerney, Sarah. "Steve Jobs: An Unconventional Leader." *Executive Style*, 2011. www.executivestyle.com.au/steve-jobs-an-unconventional-leader-1lcmo.

Nathan, Mitchell, and Karen Koellner. "A Framework for Understanding and Cultivating the Transition from Arithmetic to Algebraic Reasoning." *Mathematical Thinking and Learning* 9, no. 3 (2007): 179–92.

National Research Council. *How People Learn: Brain, Mind, Experience, and School.* Expanded ed. Washington, DC: National Academies Press, 2000.

Palus, Charles J., and David M. Horth. "Leading Creatively: The Art of Making Sense." *Journal of Aesthetic Education* 30, no. 4 (1996): 53–68.

Perlman, Adam. "Informed Mindfulness as the Foundation for Leadership." *Explore: The Journal of Science and Healing* 11, no. 4 (2015): 324–25.

Prentice, W. C. H. "Organizational Culture: Understanding Leadership." *Harvard Business Review* (January, 2004).

Rather, Dan. "ABC Nightline—IDEO Shopping Cart." *YouTube*, published December 2, 2009, by Alfonso Neri. www.youtube.com/watch?v=M66ZU2PCIcM.

Robbins, Anthony. *Unlimited Power: The New Science of Personal Achievement.* New York: Simon and Schuster, 2015.

Wallas, George. *The Art of Thought.* New York: Harcourt, Brace, 1926.

Wenger, E. C., and W. M. Snyder. "Communities of Practice: The Organizational Frontier." *Harvard Business Review* 78, no. 1 (2000): 139–46.

Wenger, Etienne. *Communities of Practice: Learning, Meaning, and Identity.* Cambridge: Cambridge University Press, 1998.

About the Author

Teruni Lamberg, Ph.D., is an associate professor of mathematics education at the University of Nevada, Reno. She received her doctorate in mathematics education at Arizona State University in 2001 and completed a postdoctorate at Vanderbilt University. She is currently an associate professor at the University of Nevada, Reno. She is the author of *Whole Class Mathematics Discussions: Improving In-Depth Mathematical Thinking and Learning* (Pearson) and coauthor of *Smarter Balanced: Grade 3* (Barron's). She is the principal investigator of the Nevada Mathematics Project.

She led a statewide initiative aimed at improving mathematics education of children through teacher training and researching the process of doing this. Her work has impacted over 12,500 students in Nevada and involved collaborating with an interdisciplinary team made up of mathematicians, math educators, scientists, cognitive scientists, the Nevada Department of Education, Regional Professional Development Program trainers, and every single school district in Nevada. Leadership skills were critical in making this project a success, and therefore she spent many years studying the business literature. This project is now formalized as an institutional initiative and got the backing of the Nevada governor's office and the State Superintendents Board of Nevada. It is now a permanent initiative of the college (www.unr.edu/education/centers/nevada-mathematics-project).

Teruni Lamberg has also held many leadership positions. She served twice as the chair of the Psychology of Mathematics Education organization for the Northern American Chapter (United States, Canada, and Mexico), a prestigious mathematics education research organization. She currently serves as the program coordinator for the STEM master's and doctoral programs at the University of Nevada, Reno. She is the director of the Nevada Mathematics Project Initiative.

Made in the USA
Las Vegas, NV
25 January 2022

42263055R00073